Alternative Schools

The Development of Options in Public Education

by

VERNON H. SMITH

School of Education
Indiana University

PROFESSIONAL EDUCATORS PUBLICATIONS, INC.
LINCOLN, NEBRASKA

Library of Congress Catalog Card No.: 74-77828

ISBN   0-88224-087-0

© Copyright 1974
by
Professional Educators Publications, Inc.

Alternative Schools

THE PROFESSIONAL EDUCATION SERIES

Walter K. Beggs, *Editor*
Dean Emeritus
Teachers College
University of Nebraska

Royce H. Knapp, *Research Editor*
Regents Professor of Education
Teachers College
University of Nebraska

Contents

1. WHY ALTERNATIVE PUBLIC SCHOOLS? 7

   Background 8
   The Paradox of Success 9
   The Situation Today 11

2. THE OPTIONAL ALTERNATIVE PUBLIC SCHOOL MOVEMENT . . 14

   What Is an Optional Alternative Public School? 14
   What Kinds of Alternative Public Schools Are There? . . . 16
   What Do Alternative Schools Have in Common? 18
   Whence the Impetus for Alternative Public Schools? 20
   The Development of Optional Alternative Public Schools . . 21
   Reactions to the Development of Optional Alternative Public
   Schools 22

3. ALTERNATIVE SCHOOLS IN ACTION 25

   Open Schools 25
   Schools-without-Walls 28
   Learning Centers 31
   Continuation Schools 33
   Multicultural Schools 34
   Free Schools 35
   Schools-within-a-School 36
   The Complex of Alternative Schools 37
   School Districts Cooperate to Develop Options 39

4. YESTERDAY'S CURRICULUM, TODAY'S STUDENT, TOMORROW'S
   WORLD 41

   Educational Taboos and Social Realities 43

The Need to Break with the Past 48
Summary 49
The Role of the Optional Alternative Public School 50

5. REFORM OR RENEWAL 52

The Need for Reform 52
What Did We Learn from Recent Reform Efforts? 53
Today, a Healthier Climate for Change 56
School Reform: How and How Soon? 59
A Strategy for Self-Renewal 59
Advantages of This Strategy 61
The National Consortium for Options in Public Education . . 64

6. OPTIONAL PUBLIC SCHOOLS: THE POTENTIAL 66

The Social Potential 67
The Economic Potential 69
The Educational Potential 70
An Idea Whose Time Has Come? 74
Afterword 75

NOTES 81

BIBLIOGRAPHY 81

CHAPTER 1

Why Alternative Public Schools?

There is, and can be, no one curriculum suitable for all time, or for all students at a given time.[1]

If there is one thing that everyone concerned with education today would agree on, it is that no single program will ever meet all of the needs of all of the students. Different children learn in different ways and at different times. Yet, for many years American public education has been attempting the impossible — to teach every child in the same way at the same time.

The basic model for public education, a single school serving a local community, was established in earlier centuries when one general store and a single public stable per community were also common. The conventional school was not designed or intended for its present responsibilities. Therefore, it is natural that public schools in this century have failed to adjust to changes in society, to changes in the culture of their communities, and to their increasingly diverse clienteles.

The public schools cater to those who learn best in traditional academic programs at the expense of those who need different learning experiences. This traditional model of schooling, which has dominated public education in this country, was imported directly from Western Europe, and was certainly not designed for a constitutional democracy. In that earlier Europe only an elite few were expected to go beyond elementary school, and one of the tasks of the school was to sift out the few who would continue in formal education. This situation still exists in many European countries.

But our society has very different expectations, based on the need for an educated electorate as the foundation of a democratic government. Earlier in this century most states made secondary education compulsory, forcing many students to stay in a system designed to eliminate them. The schools had difficulty adjusting to the responsibility for the elementary and secondary education of all children and youth.

When there is only one educational model, and that model fails to work for everyone assigned to it, the natural reaction is to try to reform the model. But many children are learning well in our traditional academic model of education, and many parents and teachers are satisfied with it. Attempts to reform or alter this basic model usually fail to consider the many who are satisfied with the status quo. This may be one of the reasons why educational reform is not always popular and why there is frequently resistance to it.

A reformed education that would meet the learning needs of all students is an impossible dream. Instead, a society that wishes to educate every citizen, needs a variety of learning models to meet a plurality of learning needs.

The development of optional alternative public schools offers a potential strategy for making schools more responsive to the needs of the students and communities they serve.

BACKGROUND

We have no option but to seek the means for making the schools more effective for all children.[2]

Following World War II (1941-45) there was increased interest in this country in the role of education. This was partly due to the growing educational needs of a technological society, and partly due to growing world competition in politics and economics. The GI Bill provided college education for many veterans who otherwise would not have been able to afford it. The result was that higher education was available to the members of all socioeconomic classes. The fifties and sixties were characterized by: (1) a growing popular interest in education in general and in the public schools in particular, (2) significant increases in the funding for public education, and (3) a burgeoning of educational innovations.

Fortunately or unfortunately, the critics of the schools captured public attention and helped to influence the popular view of the effectiveness or ineffectiveness of the schools. Dramatic criticisms of the schools appeared among the best sellers — *Why Johnny Can't Read, Compulsory Miseducation, Why Children Fail, Death at an Early Age, Our Children are Dying, Crisis in the Classroom, School Is Dead*, to mention a few with the more flamboyant titles.

When Russia launched *Sputnik*, the first space satellite, in 1957, there was a furor of concern. One of the results was the National Defense Education Act of 1958, the first massive injection of federal funds into the public schools. Congress recognized the critical importance of education in our competition with other nations while acknowledging that educational reform was essential to the national interest. During the sixties expenditures for public education increased about 250 percent, or 50 percent faster than the increase in the gross national product. Such a marked increase in funding resulted in a corresponding increase in public interest, particularly in the sectors that compete with education for public money.

Since the increase in funds for public education was closely tied to the need for reform, there was a real financial incentive for innovation. Starting with the "New Math" in the early fifties, educational innovations flourished for two decades — curricular reforms, programmed instruction, staff utilization, flexible modular scheduling, phase-elective programs, performance contracting, to mention a few.

Several recently published analyses of educational reform efforts have suggested that in spite of these two decades of reform attempts, the schools today are not significantly different or better than they were in 1950. Why did so many earnest efforts to change the schools fail to bring about significant results? Many of these attempts started with, and were dependent upon, external funding. When the funds ran out, few of the innovations survived. Some of the attempts employed a change-agent strategy. Someone from outside was going to come in and change the schools for the local community. The change-agent's perception of local needs may have been quite different from the perceptions of teachers, students, and parents. But perhaps the most significant aspect of most of these reform attempts was that they were designed for everyone. The New Math was for all students (and teachers). Flexible scheduling was for all. The schools would move from one program for every student to another program for every student. And this was an impossible goal.

THE PARADOX OF SUCCESS

Over the past decade there has been a growing awareness that public education is in trouble. The public and the profession would agree that the schools have serious problems today although they might not agree on what the problems are or which are the more serious. Whether there are more or fewer problems today than in some earlier period is not at issue here. What the public might find difficult to understand is that some of today's major problems are a result of the amazing success of public education in this country. This is the paradox. The success of the public schools in the past has created critical problems for the present. Here are some examples:

The success of the public schools created a high societal demand for education. Not long ago, if students were not doing well in school, society expected them to drop out and find something useful to do. (Remember, this reputation for success was achieved in an earlier society that offered other alternatives for youth.) Today, if students are not doing well in school, society expects the schools to change to meet their needs.

As the first nation attempting to provide free public elementary education for all children, we were so successful that society came to expect and demand mass secondary education. Public high schools, designed and developed for an elite group of students (about 6 percent graduated in 1900), are expected to accommodate 100 percent today. Even before we realized, much less solved, the problems this had created, society's expectations moved to the college level. In many communities today both white-collar and blue-collar workers expect their children to graduate from college.

The promise of continued success led to greatly increased expenditures in public education in the last decade. Congress was convinced that education was vital to the national defense, and expenditures for public education rose at a much faster rate than the growth in the gross national product. The natural result of education's getting a larger share of money was the call for educational accountability from the sectors that got a smaller share.

For some time to come, teachers, parents, and administrators will have to adjust to paradox and ambiguity, including the following:

1. The public schools are educating more students better than ever before in history, but there are more critics of the schools today, and the media make the critics far more visible and audible to the public.
2. More students are staying in school longer than ever before, but as many are dropping out today as at any previous time. More than 1,200,000 dropped out of the Class of '73 before graduation. Between 1960 and 1970 about 1,000,000 students per year dropped out of school. While this number stayed fairly constant, the percentage of dropouts was declining because the overall school-age population was increasing. There

are indications that the dropout rate has been increasing since 1970. A recent book reports that "forty per cent of all high school students drop out before graduation."[3]

3. More students in this country are learning to read better today than at any previous time; nevertheless, the criticism of the teaching of reading is at an all-time high. Incidentally, in a recent study involving 9,700 schools in nineteen countries, when comparable groups of high school seniors were compared in reading achievement, the U.S. students ranked first.[4]

4. The majority of citizens, not necessarily the majority of parents, are satisfied with the public schools according to annual polls, but many vocal minorities are very dissatisfied.

5. In spite of this general approval, it is difficult to get adequate money to operate the schools. Personal income is at an all-time high, and school-bond-issue defeats are at an all-time high.

6. The final paradox, and the one most related to the remainder of this book, is that the schools, in spite of two decades of sincere efforts to change them, remain almost as they were in 1950, or even 1900. We spent two-and-one-half-times as much per pupil in 1970 as in 1960, but we have little evidence that education was better. Some think it was worse. Education, once designed to be responsive to local needs and local control, has become a monolithic bureaucratic system unresponsive to the needs of many and even more unresponsive to change efforts.

This then is the condition which confronts us: though youth is no longer the same, and the world is no longer the same, high schools are essentially unchanged from what they were at the beginning of the century.[5]

. . . in the school culture the more things change the more they remain the same . . . [6]

THE SITUATION TODAY

Parents and educators who wish to see public education become more responsive to the needs of all children and youth are faced with a challenging situation. The residual effects of the reform efforts of the last twenty years have created the need for new strategies for reform and renewal in public education.

Throughout the past decade there has been a growing awareness on the part of the public and the profession that the schools are not responsive to the needs of some students — the dropouts, the racially and culturally different, and the poor, to name a few of the obvious groups. But a report from the U.S. Office of Education states that the schools are not responsive to the gifted.[7] And the primary impetus for the nonpublic "free" school movement of a few years ago came from white middle-class parents. There is a further general concern that today's schools are no longer adequate to meet tomorrow's needs for their clienteles and for society as a whole. Educators, particularly some of those most involved in various change efforts, are begining to realize and admit that there is little evidence indicating that anyone knows how to change the schools.

I can't present any neat solutions; nobody knows the answers.
Harold Howe,
Former U.S. Commissioner of Education[8]

I'm not sure we have any real clues at the present time on how to reform the educational system.
Paul Nachtigal
The Ford Foundation[9]

I'm fresh out of major things to look at in terms of educational reform. We sort of had the course and here are the schools just like they always were. Where do we go from here?
Dwight Allen
University of Massachusetts[10]

This is forcing those concerned about public schools to make a serious analysis of the problem. In the late fifties and early sixties all the experts had solutions. There was little concern with the problem. Once you have the vaccine, it is no longer necessary to study the disease. But we found out that many of these educational vaccines were for the symptoms, not the causes. Now it is necessary to return to a more careful study of the root problems.

There is a legitimate public concern that schools and teachers should be accountable for what they do. Whom they should be accountable to is not entirely clear. Should they be accountable to the clientele they serve — students, parents, and community — or should they be accountable to governmental agencies — state departments of education, the U.S. Office of Education, or the National Institute of Education?

One of the growing responses to educational concerns has been the search for alternatives — alternative curricula, alternative modes of instruction, alternative organizational structures, alternatives to the public schools, and even alternatives to schooling. This search for alternatives has included a growing interest in nonpublic schools and in Ivan Illich's society without schools.[11] In spite of the widespread popularity of Illich's book and of the many publications on nonpublic schools — Summerhill schools, free schools, commune schools, and various counterculture schools — these alternatives have little promise for the foreseeable future. The number of students in nonpublic schools has declined to an all-time low today and is predicted to decline even farther by 1980. For over 90 percent of the students in this decade, and perhaps in this century, the public schools will provide the sole opportunities for formal education.

The need for a plurality of modes of education to meet the needs of our diverse population has never been greater. The development of a diversity of optional public schools, each geared to be responsive to students with different learning needs and styles, provides one strategy for developing a new organizational structure for public education. The development of optional alternative public schools could provide choices for students, parents, and teachers in every community.

CHAPTER 2

The Optional Alternative Public School Movement

The development of public schools of choice is the only major movement in American Education today.[1]

The alternative school movement within public schools has grown enormously in the past 10 years.[2]

During recent years a new concept has emerged in public education. In many communities today, students, parents, and teachers are accepting and even demanding options in public education. As shown in Figure 1, the number of alternative public schools is growing rapidly. Over a thousand are currently operating in hundreds of communities in over forty states and Canada, Denmark, Norway, and Sweden. Many more communities are exploring, planning, and developing alternative public schools. These alternatives have developed with little or no communication with each other and without national or state coordination. They have not come as a response to educational crisis, but have been developed to meet specific needs within their local communities. Because each alternative has developed as a response to an individual community's educational concern rather than as a response by the mainstream of the profession to a concern for the national interest, the alternatives represent the first evolutionary thrust in public education at the "grass-roots" level.

WHAT IS AN OPTIONAL ALTERNATIVE PUBLIC SCHOOL?

As used herein, the term *alternative public school* means any school that provides alternative learning experiences to those provided

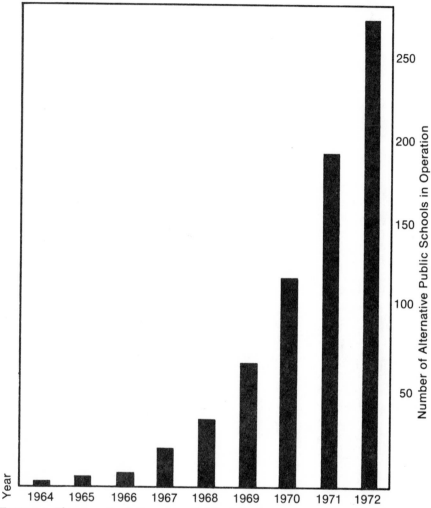

FIGURE 1. The Growth of Alternative Public Schools, 1964-72. Based on information from 276 alternative public schools. (From *Changing Schools*, No. 8, p. 5. Reprinted with permission.)

by the conventional schools within its community and that is available by choice to every family within its community at no extra cost. When a community has several optional alternative public schools available, the conventional school becomes one of the options, but for our puposes herein, the conventional school will not be included in the above definition.

WHAT KINDS OF ALTERNATIVE PUBLIC SCHOOLS ARE THERE?

Since alternative public schools usually develop as responses to particular educational needs within their communities, there is no single model or group of models that would encompass their diverse nature. However, the majority of alternative public schools fit into the following types or into combinations of these types.

Open Schools*

Learning activities are individualized and organized around interest centers within the classroom or building. While the concept of open education is not new, there has been a revival of interest in it beginning with the development of informal infant schools in Great Britain following World War II.

Schools-without-Walls*

Learning activities are carried on throughout the community and with much interaction between school and community. Philadelphia's Parkway Program, which opened in 1969, was the first and is probably the most well known of these.

Learning Centers

Learning resources are concentrated in one location available to all the students in the community. This would include magnet schools, educational parks, career-education centers, vocational and technical high schools, and similar institutions.

Continuation Schools

These schools provide for students whose education in the conventional school has been (or might be) interrupted. This would include dropout centers, reentry programs, pregnancy-maternity centers, evening and adult high schools, street academies, and the like.

*Both these terms (open schools and schools without walls) are also used for architectural concepts in school buildings. We do not so use them here. The terms refer to concepts for organizing learning activities that may be used in a diverse array of physical facilities.

Multicultural Schools

These schools emphasize cultural pluralism and ethnic and racial awareness and usually serve a multicultural student body. Bilingual schools with optional enrollment would be included here.

Free Schools

These schools emphasize greater freedom for students and teachers. This term is usually applied to nonpublic alternative schools, but a few are available by choice within public school systems.

Schools-within-Schools

A small number of students and teachers are involved by choice in a different kind of learning program. This would include mini-schools and satellite schools. A satellite school is a school at another location which maintains administrative ties to the parent school. The schools-within-schools would usually belong to one or more of the six types described above. See Figure 2.

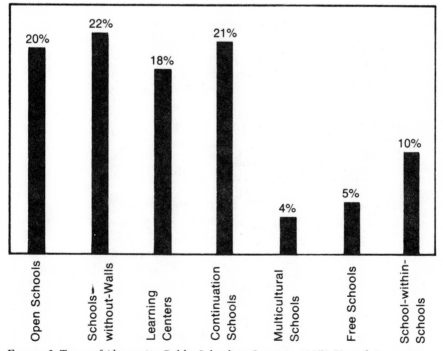

FIGURE 2. Types of Alternative Public Schools in Operation, 1972-73, with Percentages of Total. (From *Changing Schools*, No. 8, p. 6. Reprinted with permission.)

Not all alternative public schools would fall into these types. There is at least one optional alternative public school where all learning activities are based on behavior modification (Grand Rapids, Michigan) and at least one other that is a nongraded continuous-progress school (Minneapolis, Minnesota).

In addition to the functions mentioned above, many alternative public schools operate as voluntary integration models within their communities.

Special-function schools that serve students who are assigned or referred without choice are not included in this definition. A school for disruptive students may be desirable in some communities, but it should not be confused with an optional alternative public school.

WHAT DO ALTERNATIVE SCHOOLS HAVE IN COMMON?

While each alternative public school has been developed within its community in response to particular local needs, most of the alternatives share some or all of the following characteristics:

1. They provide options within public education for students, parents, and teachers. Usually these choices are open to all, but there must always be a choice for some so that the alternative schools have a voluntary clientele. There are many promising innovative schools throughout the country, but if there is no choice of schools within a community, they would not be included in the category of alternative public schools as defined herein.
2. The alternative public schools have a commitment to be more responsive to some need within their communities than the conventional schools have been.
3. The alternatives usually have a more comprehensive set of goals and objectives than their conventional counterparts. While most alternatives are concerned with basic skills development and with college and vocational preparation, they are also concerned with the improvement of self-concept, the development of individual talent and uniqueness, and understanding and encouragement of cultural plurality and diversity, and the preparation of students for various roles in our society — consumer, voter, critic, parent, spouse . . .
4. They are more flexible and therefore more responsive to planned evolution and change. Since they originated in today's

scientific age, the alternatives have been designed to rely on feedback and formative evaluation as they develop and modify their programs.

5. The alternatives attempt to be more humane to students and teachers. Partly because they tend to be smaller than conventional schools (see Figure 3), alternatives have fewer rules and bureaucratic constraints for students and teachers. In many cases the alternative has been designed to eliminate aspects of the culture of the conventional school that are most unpleasant and oppressive to its clientele and its faculty.

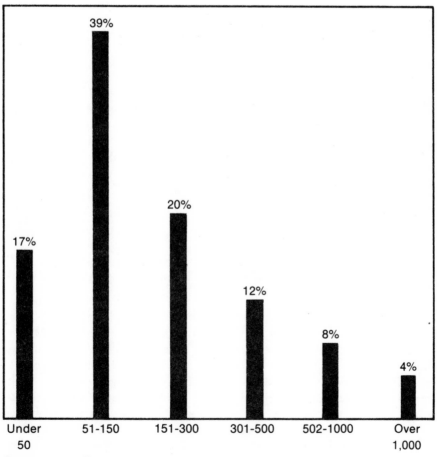

FIGURE 3. Enrollments in Alternative Public Schools, 1972-73, with Percentages of Total.

WHENCE THE IMPETUS FOR ALTERNATIVE PUBLIC SCHOOLS?

The most striking thing about the proponents of alternative public schools is their diversity. One is almost forced to conclude that the concept of options in public education is an idea whose time has come. Widespread backing for alternative public schools has emerged from a wide variety of sources, both inside and outside the profession.

National Studies on the Status of Public Education

The 1970 White House Conference on Children recommended "immediate, massive funding for the development of alternative optional forms of public education."[3] The President's Commission on School Finance recommended that "options [alternative public schools] be provided to parents and students."[4] A joint report issued in 1973 by the Educational Facilities Laboratories and the Institute for the Development of Educational Activities of the Keltering Foundation endorsed the development of optional alternative public schools.[5] An unpublished study by the Institute for Educational Development suggests a variety of alternatives that would transform public education.[6] The Association for Supervision and Curriculum Development passed a resolution in 1972 recommending alternative forms of schooling. The North Central Association of Colleges and Secondary Schools has a task force working on guidelines for the accreditation of optional alternative schools.

Governmental and Private Agencies Concerned with Educational Reform

Berkeley's alternative public schools and Philadelphia's Parkway Program started with Ford Foundation funds. The U.S. Office of Education is funding the National Alternative Schools Program at the University of Massachusetts, and multiple optional alternative schools in Berkeley and Minneapolis are currently funded through the Experimental Schools Program of the National Institute of Education. (While some alternative public schools have started with external funding, the majority have not.) State departments of education in Connecticut, Delaware, Florida, Illinois, New Jersey, New York, Pennsylvania, and Washington are encouraging the exploration and development of alternative public schools.

Local Community Groups Concerned about the Quality of Public Education

In Tuskeegee, Alabama; Malibu, California; Aurora, Colorado; Lafayette, Indiana; Sharon, Massachusetts; Ramapo, New Jersey; and over a hundred other communities; parents have banded together to encourage school boards to provide options for their children.

While public education's failure to meet the needs of the poor and the racially different is well documented, the majority of the parents who are seeking public alternatives within their communities are middle class and white.

Proponents of Other Reform Efforts See Optional Alternative Public Schools as the Key to Other Reforms

The advocates of community control see the development of options for all families as a means of local consumer control of public education. With the apparent demise of performance-contracting and the doubtful future of the voucher system, proponents of accountability in education see this same potential in consumer control through options.

Students, Teachers, and Administrators Create Their Own Alternative Public Schools

Most alternative schools develop at the grass-roots level through the combined efforts of students, teachers, administrators, and parents.

THE DEVELOPMENT OF OPTIONAL ALTERNATIVE PUBLIC SCHOOLS

There have always been alternatives to public education. We have always had private schools for those who could afford them. Vocational schools were developed in this century for those who "needed" nonacademic programs. Until shortly after World War II a student could drop out of school to take a job; therefore, work was a legitimate option for some. But changes in society have made this option available to fewer and fewer in recent years. The need for programs for dropouts and potential dropouts was recognized in the fifties and sixties, and a few dropout centers and street academies were established. Some school districts established evening high schools for adults and youths who were employed in the daytime. The magnet school concept was developed in several cities, usually for select or elite groups of students. A few school districts adopted open-enrollment policies to allow families a choice of any school within the district.

But to the media, and therefore to the public, the alternative public school began with the Parkway Program in Philadelphia in 1969. This is an appropriate birth date for the alternative public school because Parkway was probably the first public school created to be an option for any student within its community, the city of Philadelphia. Berkeley's Community High started the same year; Chicago's Public High School for Metropolitan Studies (Metro) followed in 1970; and the race was on.

The last two years have produced the development of multiple options within a single community. In Berkeley in 1972-73 all families could choose from among twenty-three alternative schools and programs plus the conventional schools. Over one-third of Berkeley's students were enrolled in the alternative schools. In the Minneapolis Southeast Alternatives families have a choice among four alternative elementary schools: the Tuttle Contemporary School, the Marcy Open School, the Pratt/Motley Continuous Progress Schools, and the Southeast Free School. On March 13, 1973, "the Minneapolis School Board voted unanimously to try to offer alternative educational styles to all elementary students in the city by the fall of 1976."[7] Philadelphia currently operates over sixty alternative schools and programs at the secondary level. In Los Angeles last year a study by students, community members, and professionals recommended twenty-five alternative schools and programs at the high school level. The Los Angeles School Board has endorsed the alternative school concept and a set of guidelines for developing alternative schools. Multiple options are currently available in Ann Arbor and Grand Rapids, Michigan; Cherry Creek and Jefferson County, Colorado; Quincy, Illinois; St. Paul, Minnesota; Cleveland Heights, Ohio; Seattle, Washington; and Madison, Wisconsin.

REACTIONS TO THE DEVELOPMENT OF OPTIONAL ALTERNATIVE PUBLIC SCHOOLS

Prior to 1970 *options* and *alternative public schools* were little talked about and seldom, if ever, referred to in the literature of education. These two terms are now so common and widespread that they are almost ubiquitous. This situation may be partly related to the search for alternatives in many other aspects of society today.

Over two hundred articles and books on alternative public schools have been published since 1970. Several professional journals have devoted feature issues to the development of alternative schools — *Educational Leadership, Harvard Educational Review, National Elementary Principal, Nation's Schools, NASSP Bulletin,* and *Phi Delta Kappan.* The American Federation of Teachers, the National Education Association, and *Education U.S.A.* have published special monographs on alternative schools. Both *Time* and *Newsweek* have had education feature stories on alternative schools. Naturally, most of the publications are favorable because most of the authors are advocates of options in public education.

When people discuss alternative public schools, the question is usually asked: How do colleges react to students who have attended alternative public high schools? Directors of alternative high schools report that when college admissions officers are informed about the school's program, admissions and placement are not problems. In Cambridge, Chicago, and Philadelphia, the alternative high schools send a higher percentage of students on to college than the conventional high schools. After Parkway's first two classes had graduated, John Bremer reported, "Every student who had applied to college had been accepted, most of them by their first choice."[8]

Teacher-Education Institutions

Teacher-education institutions have not been characterized by immediate responses to changes in the field of public education. Surprisingly, following the lead of Indiana University and the University of Massachusetts, about a dozen institutions are developing or operating programs to prepare personnel for various roles in alternative public schools. Many more institutions are currently offering courses and workshops which include the study of alternative modes of public education.

The Alternative Public School's Own Community

The critical reaction is that of the school's own community. Since the school has developed to meet local needs, the ultimate test must be its acceptability within its community. Since the alternative exists as an option, the crucial test is whether it attracts and holds students. Many alternative schools are filled to capacity and have waiting lists. In Chicago and Philadelphia thousands of students apply each year for the few hundred openings at Metro and Parkway. The Metropolitan Youth Education Center, a program for dropouts and potential dropouts jointly operated by the Denver and Jefferson County Public Schools, has served over twenty thousand students since it began in 1964.

CHAPTER 3

Alternative Schools in Action

This chapter presents brief descriptions of a few of the optional alternative public schools in operation in 1973-74. These brief descriptions will not provide a comprehensive view of the individual school, but hopefully, they will illustrate the variety of alternative public schools in operation today.

The information presented herein was gathered from several sources: visits to schools, conversations with students and staff, fugitive materials furnished by the schools, and responses to a questionnaire which was mailed to the schools. Direct quotations may come from any of these sources. If one individual was the primary source, his name is provided. Some alternative public schools have written descriptions available upon request. Some do not.

OPEN SCHOOLS

Open schools are usually organized around interest centers or resource areas and are usually characterized by flexibility in their operations. The Brown School in Louisville, Kentucky, an open school for grades 3 through 12, serves as a model for voluntary racial integration. The St. Paul Open School, which started because of the concerns of a group of St. Paul parents, enrolls students from kindergarten through grade 12.

The Brown School, Louisville, Kentucky

The Brown School opened in 1972 in the former Brown Hotel in downtown Louisville. Before the school year was over it moved into the remodeled Brown Office Building nearby. The school has an enrollment of four hundred students in grades 3 through 12. The Brown School is an open multicultural school and serves as a voluntary integration model within the Louisville community. Enrollment is open to any family in the city. Currently there is a long waiting list for admission to the school.

The curriculum is being developed around learning centers within the school and learning activities throughout the community. Students are encouraged to assume greater responsibility for their own learning as they progress through the school. Many classes are nongraded. The high school curriculum is problem-centered, drawing upon all subject-areas for solutions to existing problems.

The school population is intended to reflect the makeup of the city in terms of black-white ratio, advantaged-disadvantaged, boys-girls, and so forth.

Before the school opened, the faculty developed a philosophy, a statement of goals and a list of strategies for goal attainment. The school's philosophy follows:

The Brown School Philosophy

We believe: That man is a creative being set above and apart from all other species of living things by a compulsion to extend his powers beyond those needed for mere survival — to invent new patterns of relationships with his fellows and his environment; to generate new ideas and objects; to increase and enrich the range of available personal experience; to explore and attempt to explain the realms of the unexplainable; to view himself both in his own time and in relation to all past and future time; and to communicate to his fellows his own discoveries within his emotional, physical, social, and intellectual life.

We believe: That childhood and adolescence are the critical stages in life during which the natural creative impulse is either nurtured and developed or sublimated and subdued.

We believe: That the deliberate nurture of creativity is not only a valid but a high priority goal of education.

We believe: That the environment in the traditional school too frequently arbitrates against the development of creative powers as those powers are defined and described by contemporary learning psychologists and researchers. Elements of the school repeatedly identified as stultifying to creativity are (1) clock-dominance of learning tasks; (2) emphases on grades and competition; (3) measurement of individual progress by traditional norms, resulting in the system of promotion or failure; (4) emphases upon silence, order, and neatness; (5) teaching methods which place the learner in a passive role to receive and process information pre-selected for him; (6) the work/play dichotomy; (7) the arbitrary compartmentalization of learning into subject areas, with the subsequent learning of these subjects as ends in themselves rather than as means of illuminating life and solving life problems; and (8) physical plants which tend to limit the free flow of learning activities.

Because we further believe:

That the environment in which learning takes place determines the amount of learning, attitudes toward learning, the image one holds of himself as learner, and ultimately, the kind of person the learner becomes, the Brown School will be an alternative school for children whose parents share our beliefs regarding the importance of nurturing and developing creativity in children in a carefully planned but flexible environment.

Information furnished by Martha Ellison, Director.

The St. Paul Open School

Because a number of parents in St. Paul wanted a different education for their children, the St. Paul School Board authorized this research and demonstration unit, which opened in the fall of 1971. The school has an enrollment of five hundred students, K-12, ages five through eighteen, representative of the city's geographic areas and its citizens' socioeconomic and ethnic backgrounds. Before the end of its first year, there were 750 more students on the waiting list to get in.

Wayne Jennings, the director, states, "The Open School has chosen the toughest assignments in education—to truly individualize schooling, develop life-long learners, and make school an exciting place for every child."

The school is organized around seven major learning or resource areas: art, music-drama, humanities, math-science, industrial arts, home economics, and physical education. Each of these areas has a library-resource center and a "smorgasbord" of learning activities. Many areas have rooms for quiet study, rooms for group or individual projects, and large open spaces.

The statement of goals which follows is representative of the comprehensive goal statements that are being developed in alternative public schools around the country.

St. Paul Open School Goals

WE SEEK TO ESTABLISH A PROGRAM
IN WHICH PEOPLE:

1. Approach learning with confidence and joy.
2. See themselves as worthwhile persons.

3. Are basically comfortable but at the same time are committed to respond honestly to others' actions.
4. Have an active positive regard for every person as an individual.
5. Develop an understanding of human social systems and physical environments.
6. Develop and reassess personal values by involvement with diverse value systems.
7. Develop social skills including conciliation, persuasion, honest communication and group decision-making.
8. Develop basic skills including reading, writing, speaking, computation and learning.
9. Develop good health habits, physical fitness and recreational skills.
10. Develop willingness to take risks, participate actively even in the face of uncertainty, develop commitments and become involved.
11. Think through and deal with the possible consequences of their personal decisions and actions.
12. Develop a sense of awe and wonder; a capacity for esthetic appreciation and enjoyment.
13. Are creative, curious, open to new experiences.
14. Believe their individual actions can influence the course of events.
15. Practice and develop the ability to critically evaluate information received for use in decision-making.
16. Recognize the humor and incongruity that is a part of the human experience.

Information furnished by Wayne Jennings, Director.

SCHOOLS-WITHOUT-WALLS

The school-without-walls usually has learning activities throughout its community and interaction between school and community so that the conventional barriers between the school and its community are broken down. Each school-without-walls is unique because each community has its own unique resources. Chicago's Metro utilizes the resources of a huge urban area while City School and Walden III are based in smaller cities. Metro started with initial impetus from the central administration; Walden Three originated with a group of Racine teachers; and City School was jointly planned by students, educators, and parents.

Walden III, Racine, Wisconsin

In Racine, Wisconsin, a group of teachers from Racine High School got together to plan and develop an alternative open school without walls. The school opened in 1972 with 175 students in grades 11 and 12. The school is available by choice, to all students with parent permission.

The curriculum is cooperatively developed by "students, staff, and city life." The school uses space available in the community, including a seventy-year-old, vine-covered elementary school, a technical-institute building in the center of the city, and university-extension classrooms.

Walden III has the following comprehensive set of objectives:

I. Staff and students will participate and experiment in cognitive and affective learning experience.
   a. Students will exhibit increased ability in reading, writing, and listening skills.
   b. Students will understand the relationship between specific disciplines.
   c. Students will see positive value in school and learning.
   d. Students will study academic areas that they feel a need for further expertise in.
II. Staff and students will use the community as a major resource for the program.
   a. Business, labor, political, and educational leaders and innovators will be asked to serve as resource people for students, so that students can better understand what is needed in these areas and identify the survival skills used by the resource person.
   b. Students will become personally involved in the community by implementing and/or helping implement problem solving programs.
   c. When it is deemed appropriate by the students and staff, seminars, classes, etc. will be held in proximity to the situation under examination.
III. Students will learn how to work independently.
   a. Students will initiate, implement and be accountable for their own approaches to learning.
   b. Students will create areas of study that are relevant to their needs.
IV. Students and staff will develop skills that will help them survive in the future.
V. Students and staff will approach academic work from an emotional as well as intellectual point of view so that it has personal importance to them.
VI. All participants will develop a community of scholarship that is based on commitment to people as unique humans capable of unique responses and approaches to learning and living.
VII. Each student will attempt to teach as well as learn through facilitating new learning experiences for others. (Such as a good reader helping a poor one to read better.)

92162

   VIII. Students will examine their own value systems to see if they are
         equipping themselves for survival.
    IX. Students will participate in "real choice" situations and be held
         accountable for the consequences of their choices.
     X. Students will no longer feel disaffected from learning.
    XI. Students will examine, identify and learn skills necessary for sur-
         vival in and out of school; such as reading effectively, speaking
         effectively, learning independently, computational proficiency and
         interpersonal skills.
   XII. Students will develop a respect for life in all its manifestations, both
         human and non-human.
  XIII. Students will explore consequences of various life styles.
   XIV. Students will learn how their community works by their involve-
         ment in it with resource people and teachers.
Information furnished by David Johnston and Jackson Parker, Codirectors.

The Chicago Public High School for
Metropolitan Studies (Metro)

Metro opened in February, 1970, and was probably the third
school-without-walls in the country (after Philadelphia's Parkway
and Berkeley's Community High, which both started in 1969). Metro's
students are chosen from volunteers by a lottery to assure equal dis-
tribution from all Chicago school districts and to reflect the ethnic,
racial, and socioeconomic makeup of the city. Each year there are
hundreds more applicants than the school has spaces for.

The current enrollment is 350 students in grades 9-12, with a
staff of twenty-seven plus about thirty cooperating "teachers" who
are members of the Chicago community. The school has headquar-
ters space in a downtown office building. Classes meet in available
space throughout the downtown Chicago area.

The curriculum is flexible and innovative and provides a wide
variety of choices. Students choose from over a hundred elective
courses for each ten-week cycle. A student might select TV Production
at NBC, Creative Writing at *Playboy*, Marine Biology at the Shedd
Aquarium, or Animal and Human Behavior at the Lincoln Park Zoo.

Students and staff participate in the decision-making process.
Because Metro exists within a large, bureaucratic, urban school system, it has faced many interesting political problems. It is a tribute
to its director, his staff, and the student body that Metro has not only
survived, but continues to offer the youth of Chicago a significantly
different educational program.

Information furnished by Nate Blackman, Director.

City School, Madison, Wisconsin

City School in Madison, Wisconsin, is a school-without-walls with an enrollment of 105 students in grades 9-12. The school started in the fall of 1972 with students chosen by lottery from throughout the city. The planning group for the school was composed of high school students, teachers, community members, TTT fellows and administrators of the TTT Program (Trainers of Teacher Trainers) at the University of Wisconsin, and the director of high schools for the school system.

The school is housed in a building which also houses an elementary school, a Montessori Program, and a pre-primary program. Some of City School's students do internships in these other schools with the younger students.

The curriculum focuses on the resources of the community. In the first semester 118 courses were offered. Thirty-seven of these were taught by community teachers, including nurses, veterinarians, social workers, policemen, lawyers, and salesmen. Forty-three of the courses were internships within the community.

One of the interesting features of City School's first year is that a comprehensive evaluation was planned and implemented.

Information furnished by Conan Edwards, Administrator.

LEARNING CENTERS

Learning centers provide a concentration of resources in one location available to all of the students in the community. The Saint Paul Learning Centers Program is a voluntary racial integration model. The John Dewey High School is a magnet school for the Brooklyn community. The Skyline Center is a new educational park in Dallas.

The Saint Paul Learning Centers Program

In 1971 the Saint Paul Public Schools began to develop a network of learning centers which would provide for the voluntary integration of students. During 1971-72 the following centers were opened: the New City School Learning Center (senior high), the Junior and Senior High School Performing Arts Learning Center, the Junior High Automotive Transportation Learning Center, plus the following elementary centers: Aesthetic Environment Learning

Center, Foreign Language Learning Center, Social Environment Learning Center, the Environmental Inquiry Learning Center, Elementary Career Exploration and Development Learning Center, and the Black Minority Culture Resource Lab.

All students are assigned to their home school for basic education. Each student may elect to spend part of his school day in one of the learning centers for one quarter during the school year. "The centers are designed to attract a cross section of all children—poor, affluent, minority, non-minority, high ability, low ability, etc." All students are bussed from their home schools to the learning centers.

Voluntary participation in the learning centers program was above 90 percent. Eight thousand St. Paul students were bussed voluntarily in this program during the 1972-73 school year. By 1975-76 this program will be fully implemented and available to every family in St. Paul. It is important to note that while the Learning Centers Program is a strategy for voluntary integration in the St. Paul Schools, the choices that students and their parents make are educational; that is, they choose to attend a particular educational program.

Information furnished by Firmin Alexander, Executive Administrator.

John Dewey High School

This innovative learning center has a volunteer student body representing a cross section of the Brooklyn community. Students who live in the immediate school district have first choice. The remaining places are filled from the other areas in Brooklyn.

The school operates eight hours a day, twelve months a year. There are no grade-levels, no grouping or tracking, no Carnegie units, and no lockstep curriculum. Instead there are personalized counseling and a broad choice of course options within each subject-area. Both students and teachers are involved in the development of the educational program.

The school year is divided into five seven-week cycles with an optional sixth cycle in the summer. The school has a flexible modular schedule with emphasis on individual progress and independent study. Each curriculum area has its own resource center.

The school opened in 1969, and is currently in its fifth year of operation.

Skyline Center, Dallas, Texas

The Dallas Independent School District's Skyline Center is one of the largest educational parks in the country—a fourteen-acre building complex on an eighty-acre campus. The center is open to students from any high school in Dallas. The center's goals include extensive preparation in career education, individualization of instruction, and involvement of community. The intent of the center is to become a catalyst for positive educational change.

The center has three main divisions. Skyline High School is a comprehensive high school, grades 10 through 12, which enrolls students from outside its district when they are enrolled in the Career Development Center.

The Career Development Center provides programs which would not be feasible because of space or cost in individual high schools. For example, CDC has an aircraft hangar and airstrip, a computer center, and classes in Greek and Swahili.

The Center for Community Services provides continuing-education programs for adults and for out-of-school youths. These programs include adult basic education, distributive education, trade schools, vocational office education, and a general-education diploma program.

CONTINUATION SCHOOLS

Continuation schools provide opportunities for students whose education is interrupted to continue on for their high school diplomas. The Metropolitan Youth Education Center and Pacific Shores High School have been in operation long enough to serve the needs of thousands of students within their communities.

The Metropolitan Youth Education Center

In 1964, when many urban and suburban schools were overlooking the severity of the dropout problem, Colorado's two largest school systems, Denver and Jefferson County, cooperated in the development of the Metropolitan Youth Education Center. The center is designed for students who wish to obtain high school diplomas and for students with diplomas who wish to improve their skills for employment or college entrance.

The center opened in the fall of 1964 with thirty-two pupils at a Jefferson County location. Today, in its tenth year, it has four sites serving over two thousand students. Over twenty thousand students have attended the center, and its graduates have entered colleges throughout the country.

The school offers a wide range of academic and vocational courses on a completely individualized, tutorial basis. Metro operates with personalized counseling services and a minimum of rules. "The pupil is on the threshold of adulthood. Give him the chance to act his age." The emphasis at the center is to "provide a school to fit the needs of pupils whose own uniqueness other more conventional schools have overlooked."

The school operates on a twelve-month basis with both day and evening classes. A student may enter, interrupt, or reenter at any time.

Pacific Shores High School, Manhattan Beach, California

Pacific Shores High School, now in its ninth year of operation, started as a continuation school for dropouts in its community, Manhattan Beach, California. The school gradually evolved into an innovative alternative high school for students whose needs are not being met in the traditional school program. The school has small classes, individualized instruction, and flexible scheduling. It offers courses in every subject area plus a pre-apprentice program.

Each student works independently and receives credit when his work is completed. Instruction is individualized, and there is no competition for grades. "Success is ensured through flexibility, empathy, patience, and a maximum of individual attention."

The broad objectives of the school are based upon man's relationship to self, to others, to governments and institutions, to the universe, to nature, and to technology.

The school has an enrollment of 325 students in grades 9 through 12.

Information furnished by George E. Mahnussen, Principal.

MULTICULTURAL SCHOOLS

Multicultural schools emphasize cultural pluralism and racial and ethnic awareness. The student body usually represents different racial and ethnic backgrounds. Agora is a multicultural high school, and SAND Everywhere is a multicultural elementary school.

SAND Everywhere School, Hartford, Connecticut

The SAND Everywhere School is located in a warehouse in a predominantly black and Puerto Rican neighborhood in Hartford,

Connecticut. The school has an enrollment of 194 black and Puerto Rican children in grades 1 through 5. The school is public and all students attend by choice.

The school is an open school with its curriculum focused on four areas: math-science, human relations, language arts, and creative arts. It has many learning activities related to the outside community and thus can be described as an elementary school-without-walls. But the overall emphasis is on cultural awareness.

A special feature of the school is continuous evaluation through the use of skill sheets and feedback.

Agora, Berkeley, California

Agora started in 1971 as Community II, an alternative high school for the over one hundred students then on the waiting list to get into Community High, the first alternative school in Berkeley, California. After the school was underway, the students, primarily white, decided to rename it Agora, to adopt a multicultural identity, and to actively recruit minority-group students. In its second full year, 1972-73, Agora had an enrollment of 125 students in grades 10-12, about one-third black, one-third Chicano, and one-third white.

Much of the emphasis in Agora is on student decision-making. Student meetings are held once a week. Students may attend staff meetings whenever they wish. Students help to determine the curriculum and to evaluate the staff.

Multicultural events involving all students are scheduled throughout the year. The curriculum includes traditional subjects, multicultural subjects, and other innovations, including Harlem Renaissance, Chicano studies, black seminar, modern and Afro dance, math games, black drama, American folklore, women's study, chess, Mexican folk dance, international cooking, and human awareness.

FREE SCHOOLS

While the term *free school* is more commonly used to designate nonpublic schools, there are a few optional alternative public free schools. The emphasis is on greater freedom for students and staff. The Murray Road Annex is housed in a former elementary school while the West Philadelphia Community Free School is housed in several renovated homes in the community.

Murray Road Annex, Newtonville, Massachusetts

Seven years ago a group of students and teachers in Newton North High School, Newtonville, Massachusetts, started a satellite free school in a former elementary school building off the high school campus. The school has 115 students and eight faculty members, plus aides, interns, student-teachers, and parent volunteers.

"Murray Road provides an opportunity for students to become actively involved in and responsible for their own education and the operation of the school." Students examine their own interests and needs, plan their own programs with faculty, and evaluate their efforts to achieve their goals. The curriculum is flexible and broad.

Decisions about the operation of the school are made by students and staff in the all-school General Meeting. Enrollment is voluntary by lottery designed to get a cross section of the Newton North district population.

There are no grades. Evaluation consists of written comments by students and teachers. Transcripts consist of excerpts from these comments selected by the student and his adviser.

West Philadelphia Community Free School

Now in its fourth year, the West Philadelphia Community Free School enrolls five hundred high school students at several locations. Students are chosen by a random-selection lottery within the West Philadelphia community. The school is designed according to the Eriksen Plan for a Public Alternative School System (PASS), which is based on the cooperative efforts of various sectors of the community—the Philadelphia Board of Education, the University of Pennsylvania, and the business and residential communities of West Philadelphia.

The high school is made up of several houses (renovated homes) with no more than two hundred students per house. The educational program is nongraded and individualized. Students take basic courses in the houses and electives in the community.

SCHOOLS-WITHIN-A-SCHOOL

Many optional alternative schools operate as part of a larger conventional school. The Cambridge Pilot School occupies part of the fourth floor of a conventional high school building, while Harambee

Prep is housed in a separate location but is under the overall administration of a larger school.

Cambridge Pilot School

The Cambridge Pilot School, a school-within-a-school (Rindge Technical High School), began in 1969 as a joint effort of the Cambridge Public Schools and the Harvard Graduate School of Education. The Pilot School is an attempt to create a smaller school characterized by informal human relationships and respect for cultural diversity.

Students are chosen by lottery to represent a cross section of the city's population. The school has an enrollment of about two hundred students representing about one-fourth of the total enrollment in the Rindge Tech building.

"The school is an attempt to create a community of students, parents, and educators mutually accountable to each other for the goals, the program, and the successful operation of the school." Students, parents, and staff share in the decision-making process and in the governance of the school.

The programmatic focus is on diversity, cross-cultural education, human relationships, and individual needs and concerns. Classes are informal, heterogeneous, and, for the most part, ungraded.

Information furnished by Ray Shurtleff, Director.

Harambee Prep

Harambee Prep is a minischool, or satellite part, of Haaren High School in New York City. Harambee began as the McGraw-Hill Street Academy in 1968, a privately funded, nonpublic center for dropouts, sponsored by the New York Urban League. In 1969-70 the street academy was taken into the New York Public Schools and renamed by students and teachers.

Currently the school has 125 students and a staff of six. The emphasis within the school is on innovation and informality. The program is designed to respond to the needs of students who were unable to adjust to the large urban high school.

The students range in age from sixteen to twenty. The school is available by choice to any student in the district.

THE COMPLEX OF ALTERNATIVE SCHOOLS

A recent development in ways of offering options is the school that houses a number of minischools or alternative schools within it.

Haaren High School, Quincy II, and New School are three versions of this school of many minischools.

Haaren High School

This conventional New York City urban high school became a complex of minischools in the fall of 1971. The population of twenty-five hundred students can choose from a variety of minischools operating as separate autonomous programs within the school. The program attempts to develop better rapport among students and teachers through the small, discrete units with 125-150 students and five to seven teachers. Each minischool has a coordinator and an adviser and is under the overall supervision of an assistant principal.

Each minischool is organized around the students' primary educational or vocational interest: college preparation, aviation, auto mechanics, career models, and so forth. In each of the minischools, all the courses in all subjects are correlated with the central theme.

Quincy Senior High II

Quincy Senior High II in Quincy, Illinois, is a complex of alternative schools-within-a-school. Students, parents, and teachers choose among seven schools: the traditional or conventional school, the flexible school with flexible modular scheduling, the PIE school (Project to Individualize Education), the fine arts school, the career school, the work-study school, and the special-education school.

Efforts are made "to match each student's learning style, interest and self-discipline with a school which offers him the greatest potential for educational and personal growth."

The total high school has an enrollment of fifteen hundred students with a faculty of eighty teachers. Students who are able to choose their school "will become more satisfied, motivated, and interested" than students who are forced into a common institution. Teachers who have a choice of schools and who develop the school's program will "own a share of stock in the enterprise." As parents help their children choose a school, they become more concerned and knowledgeable about their children's schools.

New School, Cleveland Heights, Ohio

New School is a program within Cleveland Heights (Ohio) High School which will contain six schools-within-a-school. Two of these schools, called COLs (Community of Learners), were in operation in 1972-73. Each COL has 164 students plus a staff of eight. Four additional staff members provide special support so that New School's total enrollment in 1972-73 was 328 students and twenty certificated staff members.

The present high school building is being completely redesigned to provide appropriate space for New School. When completely implemented New School will have six COLs and about nine hundred students. One of these will probably be a school-without-walls meeting in off-campus space.

An interesting aspect of New School is that it is intentionally designed without a leader. Each COL, or school, develops its own individual approach to learning. The approach is determined by students and staff without designated leadership.

The New School program is under the general jurisdiction of the administrative principal of Cleveland Heights High School, who was one of the architects of the program.

Information furnished by Bill Rosenfeld, teacher.

SCHOOL DISTRICTS COOPERATE TO DEVELOP OPTIONS

Another recent development is the optional alternative school which is cooperatively developed and supported by several nearby school districts. Shantí School serving the greater Hartford region and Park School serving eighteen school districts in Kent County, Michigan, are two examples.

Shantí School

Shantí (Hindi word meaning "the peace that surpasses all understanding") is a school-without-walls serving the greater Hartford region in Connecticut and is cooperatively supported by the Hartford Board of Education and school boards in seven surrounding districts. Shantí started in the fall of 1971 after two years of consideration and planning by educators, parents, and citizens in the Hartford area.

Students may apply with parental consent. Selection is by lottery from all applicants. The school seeks a diversified student population. Students and staff participate in decision-making and policy determination. Shantí has the following objectives: (1) to provide relevant community-centered education; (2) to provide a regional urban-based program; (3) to provide wide opportunity for flexibility and individualization of programs and learning encounters within the framework of a planned and inclusive program; (4) to establish means by which the program can be of service to the broader community; (5) to establish a climate of innovation and experimentation in education.

In 1972-73 the school had an enrollment of fifty students and a staff of six. The school operates on an annual per-pupil budget of $1,000. This amount is paid by the participating school districts for each student that they send to Shantí. Provisions have been made for internal and external evaluation.

This Information came from "Shantí School Information Brochure" and from Gene Mulcahy, Director, and Geoff Thale, teacher.

Park School, Grand Rapids, Michigan

Park School, an alternative public school for pregnant students, started in 1968. Park School is an option available to students from eighteen school districts in Kent County, Michigan. The school provides junior and senior high girls, married or unmarried, the opportunity to continue their regular educational program during pregnancy and after childbirth and also offers instruction in diet, health, prenatal and child care, and counseling to assist with personal adjustment. The curriculum includes full junior and senior high programs plus classes designed to meet the student's individual needs.

While the largest percentage of students are in the fifteen to seventeen age range, there has been a steady increase in the number of students between twelve and fourteen. While only about 13 percent of the students are married, over 70 percent choose to keep their babies. Since it began in 1968, the school has served over a thousand students.

Information furnished by Robert J. Stark, Director of Alternative Education.

ALTERNATIVES TO THE ALTERNATIVES

Another interesting recent development is the evolution of second-generation alternative public schools. In one school district the first optional alternative high school provided students and teachers with an unstructured curriculum and relative freedom from conventional routines. Before the end of the first year some of the students and some of the teachers were requesting and planning another alternative high school with less freedom and more structure. The development of alternatives and the development of alternatives to the alternatives provide a potential organizational-development strategy which could make school systems more flexible and therefore more responsive to the needs of their clienteles.

CHAPTER 4

Yesterday's Curriculum, Today's Student, Tomorrow's World

Chapter 1 mentioned three historical accidents that are constraints on the public schools today: (1) the monolithic approach to learning, which assumes all students should learn in the same way at the same time; (2) the authoritarianism that allows students (and teachers) little opportunity to determine what goes on in the schools; and (3) the lack of choice in public education, which forces all the students in a designated geographic area into one school and one program. This chapter will suggest two additional constraints: (4) the social taboos that have always restricted the curriculum, and (5) the traditional academic constraints on the curriculum.

The total effect of these constraints is an ever-widening gap between the student's experiences in the school and the student's life outside the school. Many of today's students perceive little relationship between the world of the school and their present and future lives outside the school.

This gap between school and society, which has certainly existed for centuries and probably as long as there have been schools, is far more serious today than previously for two reasons. First, students are compelled to remain in school for a longer time than ever before. The school day is longer; the school year is longer; and the legal school-leaving age is higher, forcing all students to remain in school after they have reached physical maturity. Earlier in this century the majority of youth dropped out before entering secondary school, and many children of elementary school age were full-time factory and farm workers.

Twice as many youngsters (of school age) in 1903 were answering the factory whistle instead of the school bell, some of them as young as eight.[1]

Second, the world outside the school is changing more rapidly while the schools appear to be highly resistant to change. In what has been described as a "decade of curriculum reform" (the sixties), it now appears doubtful that the schools experienced signifcant change.

The new curricula and new materials that were developed over the decade with the expenditure of millions of dollars and the involvement of hundreds of teachers in institutes have not brought about a sweeping nationwide reformation in the schools.[2]

Two Worlds

This, then, is the condition which confronts us: though youth is no longer the same, and the world is no longer the same, high schools are essentially unchanged from what they were at the beginning of the century. As a consequence, many adolescents inhabit two worlds: the one outside schoolhouse walls where they exercise considerable self-determination and are involved in life-shaping decisions, and the world inside the walls where every phase of their lives is dictated. . . . The dichotomy becomes absurd indeed when advanced experience outside brings them venereal diseases in epidemic proportions, but inside, as Superintendent Kenny Guinn of Nevada's Clark County Schools put it, "They're not allowed to buy an ice cream cone with lunch."[3]

. . . on the curriculum: . . . there is no setting before the students of economic or social or political facts and of their situation within these facts, no attempt made to clarify or even slightly to relieve the situation between the white and negro races, far less to explain the sources, no attempt to clarify psychological situations in the individual, in his family, or in his world, . . . no attempt to clarify spoken and written words whose power of deceit even at the simplest is vertiginous, . . . nor to teach a child in terms of his environment, . . . nor any understanding of our delicateness in the emotions and in any of the uses and pleasures of the body save the athletic; no attempt either to relieve him of fear of poison in sex or to release in him a free beginning of pleasure in it, . . . no indication of the damages which society, money, law, fear, and quick belief have set upon these matters and upon all things in human life.[4]

Although James Agee, in the preceding passage, was describing the curriculum of a rural Alabama school in 1936, a 1973 report, *The Greening of the High School*, indicates that his observations are startlingly appropriate for today's schools. Agee was concerned with the obvious gap between the school and the lives of these poor rural children outside the school.

EDUCATIONAL TABOOS AND SOCIAL REALITIES

To determine whether Agee's concerns are still valid today, let us examine the conflict between the traditional educational taboos and contemporary social realities. The taboos of the school reflect the taboos of an earlier society. Problems arise when the taboos of the past become obstacles to effective education for the present and the future. Here are some examples.

Love and Sexuality

Sexuality is one of the established curricular taboos, and certainly it was a social taboo until very recently. Earlier in this century both men and women wore baggy swimming suits that covered most of the body. Pornographic films were confined to stag affairs. Pregnant women were rarely seen in public and, of course, were not allowed to teach in the schools. (A 1973 Supreme Court decision made it legal for teachers to work while pregnant.) Nineteen seventy-three was a vintage year for sexuality in a society with rapidly changing values. *Playgirl* sallied out to join *Playboy* on every newsstand. Calendars with male nudes in twelve poses appeared, indicating that sexism in sex is on the decline. "Topless" and even "bottomless" women serve lunch in some restaurants; massage parlors burgeon; and on nationwide TV a visitor is invited to "hump the hostess."[5] Pornography went public with X-rated films. *Deep Throat,* a film that makes the stag movies of a few years ago seem as mild as *Little Women,* grosses millions of dollars from well-mixed audiences. In the toy market Santa Claus brings the little ones dolls that urinate and dolls with modestly voluptuous breasts. While the school curriculum still wears the baggy swimming suit, network television offers children (and their parents) "marital infidelity, coupling without marriage, sexual deviation, impotency, abortion, vasectomy, prostitution, and free love."[6] These occur during "prime time." Later in the evening parents can watch more sophisticated programming.

Meanwhile, back at the curriculum, sexuality and sex education remain taboo in many communities. Literature by such established authors as Vonnegut, Dickey, Hemingway, Faulkner, and Steinbeck was banned and burned in at least one high school in 1973. How do youth learn the realities of sex? They don't. Few school districts in this country provide realistic sex education. A 1971 survey indicates that most teenage girls who have intercourse do not use contraceptives.

Girls fifteen to nineteen "often gave as their reason their belief that conception could not occur because sex was too infrequent . . . "[7] Over 200,000 school girls become pregnant each year. Twenty-five percent of all high-school-age girls are married today.[8]

The Durham Center provides an optional alternative for pregnant girls in the Philadelphia Public Schools. When a girl is pregnant, she may, if she chooses, leave her home school to enroll at the Durham Center. There she may continue her regular academic work without interruption. In addition she takes special courses in child-care and nutrition. As soon as her child is six weeks old, she may leave the baby at the center while she returns to regular classes in her home school. The pregnant girls at the center take care of the infants as part of their child-care courses. Unfortunately, because of the heavy demand, this program is only available to girls under fifteen years of age.

Either there is more pregnancy among girls aged ten through fourteen today, or pregnancy within this age group is not as well concealed as formerly.

Unless the curriculum can be freed from the sexual and sex-related taboos, many in our society will remain woefully ignorant of love and sex, birth and birth control, pregnancy and maternity, marriage and divorce, puberty and adolescence, middle age, old age, senility, and death. The *Manchester Guardian* reports that "death has replaced sex as the great taboo subject of our society."[9]

Violence and Death

Violence and death are social realities that are seldom included in the curriculum because they are considered too unpleasant for children and youth. "By age fourteen a child has witnessed the violent assault on or destruction of 18,000 human beings on television."[10] How many of these are real and how many fiction? A high school graduate in the class of 1974 may have seen television's first live coverage of a murder when he was in first grade, thanks to Jack Ruby. He probably saw news "replays" of the deaths of John Kennedy, Martin Luther King, and Robert Kennedy. He may have gotten a TV taste of college life and death at Kent State and Southern University. He could have witnessed the 1972 Olympics in living and dying color. He probably saw news reports for more than a decade on an undeclared war followed by a declared peace which did not end the violence in Southeast Asia. He saw the ultimate in the-end-justifies-the-means mentality in the fascist tactics of Weathermen and Watergate.

He lives in a society today where American parents batter, neglect, and kill their children. Estimates for 1973 indicate that there were a million-and-a-half cases of child abuse resulting in 50,000 deaths and 300,000 permanently injured children.[11] This figure is predicted to rise in 1974. No wonder more than a million children in this country run away from home each year.

Our graduate probably attends a high school where violence is commonplace.

Over 60 percent of the school systems in this country employ security guards. School police have conventions just as school principals do. . . . In some good schools students haven't entered the rest rooms for three years because they are afraid of being assaulted.[12]

The [rest room] problem is far more serious for girls than for boys.[13]

We have become concerned in recent years about assaults on teachers. The great majority of assaults in schools are on students by other students, by outsiders, and by teachers and administrators. There is no way to estimate crime and violence in the school because "there is reason to believe that fewer than 10 percent of crimes committed in school buildings, including violent crimes, are divulged."[14]

Outside the school violent crimes tripled in the last decade, and they are still on the increase today. How does the school help children and youth to live with the realities of violence and death? Will today's students be tomorrow's violent parents? Can we afford to maintain a costly taboo because death isn't nice?

Immorality in Business, Education, and Government

Do the schools prepare students to become responsible participants in our democratic society? Does the curriculum help them cope with the reality of secrecy and dishonesty in politics and government? in advertising and business? in schools and education? Secrecy and dishonesty in government did not begin with Watergate. (But Watergate certainly received more comprehensive worldwide media coverage than any previous political scandal.) "We had become somewhat inured to breaking the law," Magruder said.[15] LBJ had Bobby Baker; JFK had the Bay of Pigs; Ike had Sherman Adams. Headline, December 5, 1957: WILL EISENHOWER RESIGN?[16] There were also major scandals during the administrations of Grant, Cleveland, Wilson, Harding, Franklin Roosevelt, and Truman. The Pentagon had its papers, its huge cost overruns, and falsified reports of bombings in

Cambodia, Laos, and Florida. The FBI committed and concealed illegal break-ins and burglaries during several recent presidential administrations. Does a democratic nation need a secret police force (the CIA) to protect its security, internally and externally? Where in the schools do we prepare students to confront these problems? Or where outside the schools do they learn this? With the reduction of the voting age, most students are eligible voters before they leave grade 12.

Detroit produced unsafe school buses, wobbly car wheels, lethal gas tanks, and falsified reports on emission systems. Even the All-American Soap Box Derby had a scandal. After the fourteen-year-old winner was caught cheating, his uncle explained that "everybody's doing it."[17]

The schools had dishonesty in performance contracting and falsified records of athletes' grades. We learned that the difference between athletics and elections is that if the coaches are caught tampering with athletics, they have to forfeit the games. Where in the curriculum is the reality of secrecy, dishonesty, and immorality in contemporary life?

The Quality of Life

Two poor black girls, ages twelve and fourteen, were sterilized without their consent or that of their parents in Montgomery, Alabama, on June 13, 1973. Their mother said that she thought they were going to get "some shots."[18] Where in the curriculum are the realities of racism and sexism? of poverty and wealth? of power and powerlessness? of security and insecurity? When will the curriculum treat black history or American Indian history accurately? Where, other than through Archie Bunker, can children learn about the lack of tolerance for diversity in this country? How will youth be able to understand the growing resentment against unsatisfying and meaningless jobs in a technological society? How does the curriculum aid in the search for alternative styles of life and living? How does the rest of this small world view the American way of living? Where in the schools or in society do we study ourselves as others see us?

By age fourteen a child has seen 22,000 hours of television, including 350,000 commercials.[19] How does the school help him to understand and analyze the ubiquitous media in his environment? How can he become an intelligent consumer and a wise conserver of the world's limited resources? Outside the school sincere local and national consumer groups worry about unsafe toys (including BB guns and pick-up-sticks) while industrial pollution, ocean pollution, and the depletion of resources continue unchecked at a rate certain to change, and probably to end, the quality of life that we have known in this country since World War II. This is already happening with the energy crisis, and it appears to surprise our leaders in politics, science, and business as much as it does the person-in-the-street.

The Future

The future is both the most critical educational taboo and the ultimate social reality. In earlier societies the study of the future was restricted to the realm of religion. The task of the schools was the transmission of the past to the children of the present.

The present curriculum in most schools is pasted together out of bits and pieces left over from the last century. Its prime assumption is that the world of tomorrow will resemble the world of today. . . .

Any curriculum that is not deduced from a set of coherent assumptions about the future is irrational.[20]

In one generation the future moved from the metaphysical to the physical. Man found the power to determine his future absolutely — he can destroy himself and all life on earth. And he has a growing number of ways to do so, thanks to science, technology, and modern warfare. A society with available means of self-destruction cannot leave its future to chance. A democratic society cannot put its future into the hands of the hands of the elected or the powerful, for the future is the responsibility of every citizen.

Are today's schools only pretending to deal with the future while actually dwelling in and on the past? Is the curriculum in your school based on "a set of coherent assumptions about the future"? The central concern of the curriculum must become the future of this world and its people. Education must help children and youth to learn to control their futures: to plan, design, and select from among various alternative futures.

In summary, these five brief illustrations indicate some of the obvious gaps between the world of the school and the world outside the school. At present we are asking future adults, who will have to confront these five issues and many more, to spend thirteen years in the public schools to prepare for adult life, but even a simple analysis reveals that the schools are not facing crucial issues of contemporary life. What the schools did in the past is not what the schools should be doing today.

THE NEED TO BREAK WITH THE PAST

It is to be supposed that all would have gone well forever with this good educational system if conditions of life in that community had remained forever
the same. But conditions changed, and life which had once been so safe and
happy . . . became insecure and disturbing.[21]

. . . a sad situation and one not susceptible to treatment by modern educators.[22]

We have moved into a period in which the break with the past provides an
opportunity for creating a new framework for activity in almost every field—
but in each field the fact that there has been a break must be rediscovered. In
education there has been up to now no real recognition of the extent to which
our present system is outmoded.[23]

The main idea is that we have moved rapidly from a period when young
people went to work fairly quickly after they became physically able to work.
Now they are held out [of productive work] in special institutions. These
special institutions are schools, and young people have the special role of
students. We do not think this special role prepares them for being adults.[24]

Children enter school with different perceptions and different expectations.
A level of teaching that was acceptable to older generations, who had no
standards of comparison, dissatisfies the children of the television age, bores
them and offends them. They are in all probability infinitely more ready to
learn than earlier generations were.[25]

Any successful institution relies on the processes that led to its
perceived success. The schools are no exception. Historically, one of
the major tasks of education was the transmission of information and
knowledge. James Coleman has pointed out that "schools as they now
exist were designed for an information-poor society."[26] The role
of the school as information-dispenser has gradually become obsolete.
At the beginning of this century there was no television, no radio,
no films, no tapes, no records, few newspapers and fewer popular
magazines, no comic books, few children's books, and even few books
in print by today's standards. Society was information-poor. By comparison the school, even with its limited supply of textbooks, was
information-rich. Where else could one learn about flax?

Flax is what school is all about. In my own old-fashioned geography books I
went to various countries in the company of Bedouin and Greek and Turkish
kids and the thing that most remains in my mind now about those imaginary

kids is that they always grew flax. I myself put flax on my maps alongside corn and wheat and coal; I wrote down flax to answer questions about the products of countries. I never knew what flax was, but I knew that if I kept it in mind and wrote it down a lot and raised my hand and said it a lot, I would be making it.[27]

The media have won the race to dispense information, but the school ignores this and keeps on running. While students observe the exploration of the moon on television, the school dispenses flax.

In earlier societies adults possessed more information than children. One of the ways for children to gain knowledge was to question adults. Those of you who are parents of school-age children probably realize that this is no longer a completely valid and reliable way of gaining knowledge. My generation was the first generation of parents and teachers to have trouble proving it possessed much more accurate information than its children and its students. The student who watches Jacques Cousteau on television knows more about some aspects of marine biology than his biology teacher—unless the biology teacher also watches Jacques Cousteau.

What is the role of the school (or of education) in an information-rich society? Coleman suggests that the society is "action poor," that the contemporary environment is particularly lacking in opportunities for children and youth to develop social responsibility and to participate in cooperative projects.[28]

SUMMARY

These five historical constraints—(1) the monolithic approach to learning, (2) authoritarianism, (3) lack of choice, (4) social taboos, and (5) the conventional academic (fact-dispensing) program—all inhibit the development of appropriate and effective programs in elementary and secondary schools.

The Juvenilization of the Secondary School

A sixth constraint affects the secondary school much more than the elementary school. Students today reach physical maturity earlier than their parents did and much earlier than their grandparents did. Yet in many secondary schools these young adults are treated as if they were incapable of making even minor personal decisions: what to wear, length of hair, length of skirt, ice cream with lunch, to list but a few. Even today, several years after the courts granted students the same rights as other citizens, some schools are accepting the decisions reluctantly, and some are not accepting them at all.

THE ROLE OF THE OPTIONAL
ALTERNATIVE PUBLIC SCHOOL

Many who have recognized the problems inherent in these constraints have concluded that the system of public education is in need of massive reform. Perhaps it is, but major reform seems unlikely to occur immediately or even in the near future. Those who are concerned about the need for more effective schools must consider other alternatives to major reform.

The development of optional alternative public schools is one such alternative. The role of the alternative public school as an attempt at major reform is doubtful at this time. Rather, the alternative school is seen as a way of complementing the conventional schools to help the total system become more responsive to some students. The cooperative development of alternative public schools within a community would provide a forum for the consideration and analysis of the aforementioned constraints. Because they are smaller, and therefore more flexible, alternative schools could be expected to minimize or eliminate some of these constraints.

Edward J. Meade of the Ford Foundation's Public Education Division summed up as follows what is "actually offered to students by the proposed alternatives that conventional schools seem not to be doing":[29]

1. Greater participation by students in decision-making about their schools and the modes of their own education.
2. More freedom of choice and more responsibility for their own work.
3. Working with a range of adults and kids of other ages.
4. Teaching other kids.
5. Serving in the community and holding jobs.
6. Spending more time by themselves.
7. Working more in groups than in classes.
8. Getting paid for work, with the school's sanction.
9. Enrolling in smaller "schools."

While most of the alternative public schools in operation today would not offer students all the features on Meade's list, all of the alternative schools would offer some of these features. Almost all of the alternative schools are smaller than the conventional schools within their communities, and almost all offer greater participation in decision-making. The student and his family had an initial choice of whether to attend the alternative rather than the conventional school. Once enrolled in the alternative the student will typically find: more opportunities for making decisions on his learning experiences, more opportunities to learn outside of formal classes, more opportunities to work with a broader range of adults and peers, more opportunities to participate in determining the rules and policies of the school, more opportunities to examine the taboos of society and education, and more opportunities to choose learning experiences outside the conventional academic curriculum.

In some alternative schools students have opportunities to learn in the community outside the school, opportunities for outside work experience (paid or unpaid) which will also count as learning experience within the curriculum, and opportunities to teach others.

Certainly, some conventional schools offer many of these opportunities. But the great majority do not offer many, if any.

The alternative school can be cooperatively designed to offer learning experiences wanted by some families but not available in the conventional school. Some of these experiences could never be offered in the large conventional school simply because the planning and logistics would require too much time, energy, and other resources. Because they are smaller, the alternative schools can try many new types of learning experiences that might not be feasible in the larger conventional school.

CHAPTER 5

Reform or Renewal

In recent decades, we have asked schools to grapple with our monumental social problems: poverty, alienation, delinquency, and racism. Schools have become central to our national defense and to the frenetic growth of the great society. We have asked schools to educate everyone and, simultaneously, to develop the maximum potential of the individual child. . . . We are expecting an educational system rooted in the nineteenth century to solve twentieth and twenty-first century problems.[1]

Of all that is uncertain about the future, one thing is clear: today's schools will not serve tomorrow's needs.[2]

THE NEED FOR REFORM

Chapter 1 mentioned the educational-reform efforts of the last two decades, their impossible goal, which was the reformation of the schools for everyone, and the growing awareness that no one really knows how to change the schools. In this chapter, we will consider the status of educational reform today and the role of alternative public schools in reform efforts for the future. Whether or when major educational reforms will occur provides a challenging topic for thought and discussion. But the probability of major reform in this decade, or even in this century, seems slight.

Yet the need for reform is well documented. Most educators and most parents would agree that the quality of education for all students could and should be improved. Most would also agree that today's schooling is inadequate to meet the needs of tomorrow's society. Further, there is little doubt that public education is completely failing to meet the needs of some students. Sidney Marland, when he was U.S. Commissioner of Education in 1971, stated that the schools were failing to meet the needs of 18-20 percent of the students. Jerome Bruner said one-fourth; Mario Fantini and Milton Young said one-third; and John Goodlad indicated that the figure might be as high as one-half.

Although the United States is well into a technological revolution far greater than the industrial revolution which preceded it, its education systems are still mired in conformity and bureaucracy. Schools are failing to educate one-third of their students and to develop the potential of most of the others.[3]

. . . it [American education] had passed into a state of utter crisis. It had failed to respond to changing social needs, lagging behind rather than leading. . . . It crippled.the capacity of children in the lowest socio-economic quarter of the population. . . . [4]

Bruner's statement, just above, is particularly interesting because his book *The Process of Education* (1960) set the tone for many of the attempts at curricular reform in the sixties. As Peter Schrag wrote in the fall of 1970, "It is ten years later and the great dream has come to an end. We thought we had solutions to everything. . . ."[5]

WHAT DID WE LEARN FROM RECENT REFORM EFFORTS?

Chapter 1 mentioned several of the common characteristics of the change efforts of the sixties: the innovations were usually intended for all students; they frequently depended on external funding; and they usually employed an intervention strategy (see Chapter 1). From these unsuccessful attempts we learned that changing the schools was far more difficult than anyone had anticipated.

This experience again pointed out the difficulty of changing a very entrenched system which apparently has an endless capacity to absorb efforts designed to improve its operation. I'm not sure we have any real clues at the present time on how to reform the educational system.[6]

The Foundation and much of the nation still held the attitude of the 1950's: innovation was regarded as stylish and even as an end in itself rather than as a means to a more crucial overhaul.[7]

Innovations without Change

We learned that there could be an amazing array of "successful" educational innovations without any significant or lasting changes in the schools. Almost every attempted innovation was a "success" as reported by its fundees to its funder. These reports, usually positive and overly optimistic, overestimated the value and generalizability of the results. The net effect of so many "successful" innovations was to create an illusion of progress and change when, in fact, there was little or no progress or change in the great majority of classrooms. Schrag blamed part of the responsibility for this illusion on the educational press. "The greatest failure of American educational journalism in the last decade is that its practitioners refused to believe what they saw, and reported instead what they were supposed to see."[8] There was too little concern for objectivity and honesty in reporting and for evaluation of funded projects by external agencies. The need for both is obvious now.

Jet-Age Research, Covered-Wagon Education

It is difficult to assess the exact status of educational progress and educational research. If the basic mode of schooling has remained relatively unchanged for over a century, as many claim, then education and educational research may still be in the covered-wagon stage. Research and innovation may produce better covered wagons, but they are unlikely to produce the automobile or the jet. The first time the horse and the automobile raced, the horse won. If that first race were to be run today according to educational research models, we would schedule three races at three different sites with internal and external evaluators, and declare the horse superior in speed for all future generations.

The methodology and technology of research today are quite sophisticated. The effects of jet-age research on the covered wagon are difficult to determine. Does sophisticated scientific research methodology aid or impede progress in education? Between 1964 and 1974 the U.S. Office of Education spent more than $200 million on educational research. In 1974 the General Accounting Office reported "little evidence of significant impact [of this research] to classrooms."[9] (This raises two questions, one about the appropriateness of USOE research and another about the appropriateness of GAO evaluation.)

With our relatively primitive level of knowledge about effective schooling, more might be learned from the careful and accurate documentation of failure than from success, whether real or imagined. Sometimes it is possible to determine the exact cause of failure, while it is usually difficult and sometimes impossible to analyze the various components of success. Educators only began to realize the value of documenting the failure of reform efforts after the publication of *Behind the Classroom Door* by Goodlad and Klein (1970), *The*

Culture of the School and the Problem of Change by Sarason (1971), and *A Foundation Goes to School* by Nachtigal (1972).

Experts without Expertise

We learned that there could be a lot of experts and a dearth of expertise. No one today really knows how to change a school significantly and permanently. Even John Dewey started his own school, which is much easier. He didn't attempt to change an existing one.[10] Expertise in education, as in other fields, has some obvious characteristics which limit its value in confronting problems arising from rapid change and discontinuity with the past.

1. Expertise was generated in, and is therefore highly dependent upon, the past. Once established, it becomes self-perpetuating.
2. Expertise accepts a responsibility for the status quo and has a vested interest in linear continuity.
3. Experts have a restricted universe of alternative futures for education. The futures they are likely to conceive will be based on linear continuity with the present and past.
4. Expertise would categorically reject futures divorced from itself, i.e., futures that deny or ignore established expertise.

Inviting an expert to help design a new school is somewhat akin to inviting the people who designed the Edsel to help design a new auto.

The Model School Concept

We learned that the model school is as likely to have a negative influence on change as a positive one. In the sixties there was increased interest in the experimental or model schools approach. A model school which would have generalizable and lasting effects on the schools of the future could be designed, developed, and tried today. This now seems doubtful for at least three reasons:

1. Professionals not involved in designing, developing, or trying the model usually have a negative view of it. The typical attitude of the staffs of conventional schools toward the model school is: "If we had just gotten all that money, all those resources, and all that attention, we would *really* have done something."

2. We are no longer sure about the transferability of the model school. One community's successful model may not be successful, or may not work at all, in another community.
3. Models sometimes generate antagonism within the community, and this may prevent them from being successful. Many parents are satisfied with the present model and do not want their children in a new one. Unless the model school is an option, it may just arouse antagonism and eventually fail, prematurely killing a potentially useful idea.

TODAY, A HEALTHIER CLIMATE FOR CHANGE

Public education entered the decade of the sixties with solutions and exited with the realization of serious unsolved problems. Today educators are taking a serious look at these problems. Fortunately, much was learned from the unsuccessful reform attempts of the last two decades. We learned that it is extremely difficult to change the bureaucratic structure of the school system, the institutional mechanisms of the school, and the traditional milieu of the classroom. We learned that there is a dearth of research on educational change, a lack of accurate institutional memory, a failure to record operational experience accurately, particularly failure, and institutional pressures to report falsely optimistic experimental results which act to conceal the need for serious reform, thereby creating the illusion of progress and change.

Typically, reform efforts focused on the modification of existing structures. The conceptualization of new structures and their subsequent trial was relatively neglected.

. . . we have been wasting our time. Despite decades of talk about "articulating" the units of public education, this objective has never been achieved because it cannot be achieved. We have simply squandered our time and energy on refining the errors inherent in the graded school when we should have thrown away the "graded" and "segmented" concept years ago.[11]

Today there seems to be a general willingness on the part of the educational profession to accept an uncomfortable situation, which includes the need for change, the lack of change in recent years, the lack of data or knowledge on change, the failure of change strategies, and the absence of new strategies for the immediate future.

The Responsibility for Change?

Teachers imagine that they determine nothing. After all, who built the school? Not the teachers. Who decided that there would be thirty-eight desks in each room? Not the teachers. . . . The principal? But the principal tells us at faculty meetings that this is the situation, he didn't invent it, we all must only live with it. The superintendent? He gives us an inspiring speech on opening day, but beyond that he makes it clear that our problems are not his invention. . . . Nobody, it seems, made any of these decisions. The people responsible for decisions about how schools ought to go are dead. . . .[12]

Rethinking Our Decisions . . . men have the opportunity to remake *all* previous decisions. Every single decision governing a school was made at one time or another by a man or by men. At the time the decisions were made, less data were available than are available today. The men who made the decisions were no brighter than we are, and they were less well educated. Therefore it behooves us to examine every decision about schooling before we make it—decisions on size of buildings and whether or not we want one at all; number of teachers and whether we need a certified teacher for every 28 and a half youngsters; whether there will be a library that houses real books, or one which is a computerized box.[13]

Herndon and Goodlad point out one of the problems that will have to be confronted in future attempts to change public education. Who is responsible? The present system fails to assign direct responsibility for learning. The recent move for accountability makes this responsibility even more remote by assigning it to state legislatures and state departments of education. Why shouldn't individual schools be directly responsible to the families they serve and to their local communities?

The single school . . . is the largest organic unit for educational change. All the rest is superstructure. . . .[14]

The Myth of Local Control of Education

From the layman's view, the educational organizations which are supposed to serve him and his children have expanded to the point where they frequently are uncontrollable. Whether it be the central office downtown, or his local school, whether it be administrators or teachers, he is outnumbered; he does not understand the issues, he does not possess the expertise to deal with the professionals, and he feels excluded from participating in decision making.[15]

We cling stubbornly to the notion of virtue in local control of education while allowing, through sheer omission, the most important decisions of schooling to be made by remote and impersonal curriculum planners who have been successful in securing National Science Foundation funds or other grants to support their work.[16]

Despite the enrollment of a sizable minority of children in nonpublic schools, elementary and secondary education in the United States is, for all practical purposes, a public monopoly. . . . The sole course available to most families is to send their children to the public school designated by the local school board. Nor in most school districts, and particularly in large cities, can a parent exercise any effective influence on what his child learns, how he is taught, or how he is treated as a person in the public school he is required to attend. One need not be an enemy of public education to agree that the stimulus of real competition might produce more responsiveness and faster responses than years of public discussion and political pressure have so far achieved.[17]

As schools and school systems have increased in size, local control has become more myth than fact. The preceding three quotations indicate a second problem that must be confronted by educators, parents, and other interested persons. As we attempt to change the schools, will we move farther away from or back toward local control of the school? Local control is far more complex than the community-control movement of the sixties assumed.

The Evaluation Myth

An interesting ritual in present-day public education requires that any new program be thoroughly evaluated. This is certainly in keeping with an age of technology and accountability. But concealed behind the ritual is an assumption that all conventional practices in education were evaluated at some earlier time and judged effective. This assumption is simply not true. And this ritual, logical as it may be, ignores what is known about the development of new concepts in education or in other fields.

We have made too few demands on old educational ideas and practices, meanwhile discouraging or even killing new ideas by premature judgment. It is clear that American schooling desperately needs new approaches to old problems, that change is exceedingly difficult, that formative must precede summative evaluation, and that innovations are fragile. Instead of putting the new to the test of fire, we should be fostering it with tender, loving care.[18]

New concepts in schooling and learning require tender nurture and sympathetic understanding rather than hostility and objectivity. If students, parents, and teachers are willing to try a new concept, and if, during that trial, they are satisfied with it, how can anyone else determine that this experience is less effective than the conventional? The application of standardized tests designed and developed for the conventional mode of education is both inappropriate and biased.

When, and if, significant changes arrive, they will probably be recognized as such and demanded by students, teachers, and parents. Meanwhile, whether early formal evaluation should continue to be used to make judgments on insignificant innovations is doubtful.

SCHOOL REFORM: HOW AND HOW SOON?

Thus far in this chapter we have discussed briefly the need for educational reform and a few of the problems related to reform. Now it would be nice to be able to report on an exciting array of strategies for immediate reform. But the situation in mid-1974, as we view it, suggests that major reform will not come in this decade, and in all probability, not in this century. By major reform, we mean some universal change in conventional schooling which would result in significant differences in all the classrooms for all the students.

Professional educators, parents, and others concerned about the need for a more effective system of public education are not likely to discover or invent the panacea they seek. Instead they will have to settle for the relatively random and sometimes haphazard development of alternative modes of education which meet particular needs perceived within individual communities. If the local development of alternative schools continues, and we believe that it will, this response will have distinct advantages over the panacean reform that many have been, and still are, seeking.

A STRATEGY FOR SELF-RENEWAL

Among the futurists there seems to be agreement that the educational systems of the future will have to provide a wide range of learning options for all citizens. Since the widespread but scattered development of individual alternative public schools does not promise major reform, we consider it a promising strategy for self-renewal in public education, which will provide a foundation for the learning options that will inevitably be required in the future. The development of optional public schools within the system is a simple and effective way to provide a total educational program that is more responsive to the needs of more families within any community.

John Goodlad has been quoted frequently in this chapter because for more than a decade he has been a national leader in the search for better schools. His book, *Behind the Classroom Door* (with M. Frances Klein and associates), published in 1970, was a landmark report proving that the innovations so widely publicized in the sixties were not affecting the vast majority of classrooms in this country.

The following quotations from Dean Goodlad were selected because the sequence of thought they present may be of interest to readers of this book:

Nevertheless, many of our schools differ markedly from what they were even a decade ago. Greatly significant changes have occurred in the curriculum and a massive reformulation of what is to be taught and learned in our schools is underway.[19]

. . . the incidence of nonpromotion, dropouts, alienation, and minimal learning in school is such that one is led to conclude that today's schools are obsolescent. They were designed for a different culture, a different conception of learning and teaching, and a different clientele.[20]

One conclusion stands out clearly: many of the changes we have believed to be taking place in schooling have not been getting into classrooms; changes widely recommended for the schools over the past 15 years were blunted on school and classroom door. Second, schools and classrooms were marked by a sameness regardless of location, student enrollment, and "typing" as provided initially to us by an administrator.[21]

Perhaps the most telling observation about our educational system is that there is not, below the level of intense criticism and endless recommendations for improvement, any effective structure by means of which countervailing ideas and models may be pumped in and developed to the point of becoming real alternatives. Stated conversely, the system is geared to self-preservation, not to self-renewal.[22]

The mere availability of a broad range of options will signify what we believe will be an important and essential change in our national value system. . . . We are at a time in history when the need to break out of established patterns is critical. We need alternatives wherever we can find them.[23]

ADVANTAGES OF THIS STRATEGY

This strategy of developing optional alternative public schools locally has several distinct advantages over other change strategies and particularly over strategies that attempt major educational reform.

Immediate Impact

Any community can plan and develop one or more optional alternative public schools. Unlike major reforms, which may require years of planning and development, the alternative-school strategy requires less planning and more action. In many communities parents, teachers, students, and others have gotten together to plan and develop a school that could become operational in the next school year. Adequate planning time will certainly vary from community to community and may take from a few months up to as much as two years.

But contrast this with the time required for major reform. Several recent national reports have suggested that the reform of secondary education must including the lowering of the compulsory attendance age to fourteen. Imagine how long it might take to convince the public and the profession that this change is desirable and then to get state legislatures to pass new attendance laws. It seems unlikely that this could occur within five years, and certainly it could take ten or more.

Another of today's suggested reforms is the development of Competency-Based (or Performance-Based) Teacher Education (CBTE).

The long-range promise, and ultimately the only justification for CBTE, is to improve the quality of instruction in the nation's schools as a consequence of improved teacher education. . . . The long-range impact of CBTE on the nation's schools is not likely to be felt for at least 10 years. . . . [24]

Won't it be difficult to generate enthusiasm for reforms that may take years to reach fruition? Because the alternative-school strategy is expedient, practical, and accomplishable within a shorter time, it should attract more enthusiastic local support. The educational changes that a community desires can be translated into immediate action.

Community Involvement

When teachers, parents, students, administrators, and others consider the need for alternatives, their cooperative involvement provides a local forum for rethinking educational decisions. By involving all the diverse elements within any community in this process, the dialogue can have parity without consensus. Since only those who wish to would select the alternative school, there is no need for consensus in planning and development. The primary concern within a community would probably be to develop alternatives for those to whom the conventional schools are least responsive. Those who are satisfied with the conventional would not be threatened by alternatives for those who aren't.

This within-community planning and development is quite the opposite of reforms based on intervention and change-agent strategies. The process is community-centered; involvement is by choice; and the purpose is to develop a response to educational needs perceived within the community. The development of alternative schools is dependent upon the expertise of local community members and local teachers and administrators. The result is local responsibility. No one else did it to or for the community.

Consumer Accountability

The alternative school has built-in evaluation and accountability. Its clientele chooses it voluntarily—or does not choose it. The development of optional alternatives within the community creates an open market, and the consumer (the family) is the judge. If no one chooses a particular alternative school, or if it is chosen only by very few, obviously that alternative is inappropriate for that community at that time. Most alternative schools have been developed to meet local educational needs, and typically the alternative school is filled to capacity and has a long waiting list. Since thousands of families apply each year for the two hundred openings in the Parkway Program in Philadelphia, that alternative must be meeting a real educational need in that community. What better accountability could anyone expect? How different this is from assigning all the children in one neighborhood to an experimental or model school, whether their families want them there or not.

Low Cost—No Cost

In general, alternative public schools operate on the same per-pupil budgets as other schools at the same level within the same community. Some cost more, and many cost less, but in most communities conventional schools also vary somewhat in per-pupil cost.

Sometimes modest funds are necessary for planning and development; sometimes they are not. As a school district moves to alternative schools, there will probably be transitional expenses just as there are always added expenses each time a new conventional school is opened. In many communities school boards and school administrators have found ways to provide alternative schools without significant expense.

Low Risk—No Risk

When we forced all students into the new programs of the sixties, many parents were unaware of the risks involved. Today, many more are aware of these risks, and there will be increased resistance to attempts to force all students into a single program.

. . . it is of critical importance to the mental health of young children for teachers and administrators to recognize that the typical new math program is appropriate for perhaps only the top third of the children—those of greatest ability to do school-type learning. Highly formalized programs are of questionable appropriateness to the middle third of the children, and clearly inappropriate, perhaps even harmful, to the self-concepts of children in the lowest third.[25]

When parents have a choice, and when they realize that the conventional school will still be available if the alternative proves to be inappropriate for their child, they will be much more willing to try new programs.

Increased Commitment to Learning

There is a loyalty to that which is chosen over that which is compulsory. Compelling people to try new programs breeds resistance on the part of some. While choice may not produce loyalty in all cases, it will certainly reduce resistance. Students, teachers, and parents will have different attitudes when they have a choice of learning experiences within the community. As soon as the alternatives develop, the conventional school becomes one of the options, and it too will benefit from a voluntary clientele.

A Transitional Structure

Attempts at reform have generally accepted the basic bureaucratic structure of public education and the one-school-per-neighborhood concept, but some educators feel that structural reform in public education is inevitable. While the initial development of alternative schools will not affect the bureaucratic structure of educational systems, it will, nevertheless, provide a structure for the incorporation of alternative modes of education into the present system.

Since the alternative schools tend to be smaller, they may lead to eventual administrative and structural changes. The energy crisis has forced Americans to become more conscious of the size of automobiles and the relationship of size to fuel consumption. A similar concern for the size of schools and the relationship of size to energy-consuming bureaucracy may develop as communities search for optimal school size and appropriate administrative structures.

THE NATIONAL CONSORTIUM FOR OPTIONS IN PUBLIC EDUCATION

In 1971, after several meetings of educators involved in the development of optional alternative public schools, the National Consortium for Options in Public Education (NCOPE) was established. NCOPE is an ad hoc group of people and institutions which seeks to encourage the development of options (alternative public schools) in public education in this decade. By 1974 the consortium had over five hundred members from over forty states, five Canadian provinces, Australia, Denmark, England, France, Germany, Norway, and Sweden, representing several hundred individual alternative public schools, plus public school systems, teacher-education institutions, state departments of education, individual students, teachers, and administrators, community groups and individual community members, education-related organizations, foundations, and other interested individuals and groups.

The consortium, with executive offices at Indiana University's School of Education, publishes a newsletter, *Changing Schools,* and acts as a clearinghouse for information on alternative public schools. The consortium sponsors regional conferences throughout the United States and Canada and plans program sessions for national educational conventions. Over a thousand persons attended the consortium's First International Conference on Options in Public Education in Minneapolis in the fall of 1973.

The consortium also provides consultant services, intervisitation arrangements, personnel exchange, and other services to its members.

Many of the members of the consortium were engaged in various efforts to reform public education in the sixties. They now believe that this development of optional alternative public schools provides the most promising strategy for educational renewal in this decade. While recognizing that the thousand-plus alternative public schools in operation today have not yet had significant effects on the mainstream of public education, advocates of alternatives believe that the development of options has significant educational and social potential.

CHAPTER 6

Optional Public Schools:
The Potential

All of the reforms that will take place in education in the next decade will have their origins in the alternative school movement.[1]

The public mood is one of willingness to acknowledge failure and to consider alternative modes. . . . [2]

Throughout the country today, practical, hard-headed educators who still believe that education can make a difference in the lives of children are operating schools different from most conventional schools. . . . Optional alternative schools represent an effective change mechanism for public education.[3]

It no longer seems necessary to justify the existence of optional alternative public schools. They appear to be here to stay. The exact role they will play in the future of public education is far from certain. Earlier in this book we mentioned that several recent national reports on education had recommended the development of alternative public schools. The most recent of these is the *Report of the National Commission on the Reform of Secondary Education*, which urges that "each district should provide a broad range of alternative schools and programs so that every student will have a meaningful educational option available to him."[4] These reports all suggest that the alternative schools will not be in competition with the conventional school, but rather that they will be complementary to the conventional school, thereby creating a total system more responsive to the needs of various clienteles and more responsive to rapid social change. This expanded system will have greater potential for meeting the future needs of our postindustrial, democratic society than the present restricted system.

THE SOCIAL POTENTIAL

All that has been said of the importance of individuality of character, and diversity in opinions and modes of conduct, involves, as of the same unspeakable importance, diversity of education. A general State education is a mere contrivance for molding people to be exactly like one another; and as the mold in which it casts them is that which pleases the predominant power in the government — whether this be a monarchy, a priesthood, an aristocracy, or the majority of the existing generation — in proportion as it is efficient and successful, it establishes a despotism over the mind, leading by natural tendency to one over the body. An education established and controlled by the State should only exist, if it exist at all, as one among many competing experiments, carried on for the purpose of example and stimulus to keep the others up to a certain standard of excellence.[5]

The great dream of universal opportunity originated in an era of social alternatives, when schooling was one of several options for advancement; the school therefore could demand certain kinds of conformity. Individuality and pluralism could take refuge and sustenance elsewhere. But for the moment all advancement begins in school, and we are, for this reason if for no other, no longer an open society. By definition, no society with but one avenue of approved entry into the mainstream of dignity can be fully open. When that single instrument of entry is charged with selecting people out, and when there are no honorable alternatives for those who are selected out, we are promising to all men things that we cannot deliver.[6]

A major characteristic of the American culture is that it is pluralistic. If pluralism means anything, it means the availability of options. Where there are no real options, you have a fraudulent pluralism — the name without the reality. This is true in business, as well as in government. It is also true in education.

At present our educational system is monolithic. One has no choice but to accept the sole approach to learning offered by the schools. The situation, if not un-American, is not American in spirit.[7]

The task is to move from educational routes which are largely characterized by bureaucratic procedures that sort students into the channels of the technical-industrial system into an educational panorama providing many avenues toward many kinds of personal and social development and which, through its pluralism, leads the other aspects of the society toward a world of alternatives and commitment to social improvement.[8]

Each of these four quotations considers the complex relationship between a democratic society and its educational system. They indicate that alternative modes of public education are consistent with a democratic philosophy, a pluralistic society, and an open-market economy. Freedom and diversity are as desirable in education as they are in other aspects of a democratic society. Giving families the freedom to choose from among educational options in an open public market would indicate a healthy democratic and pluralistic society.

The development of optional public schools within a community provides opportunities for community involvement in educational decision-making. Community boards are an integral part of alternative schools in Berkeley, Bloomington, Louisville, and St. Paul.

Since the alternative school is an option within its community, it does not require consensus to justify its existence. The alternatives can be developed to be responsive to the needs of minorities within the community. The alternative public schools may eventually provide for a range of learning styles and a diversity of value systems.

I would like to see schools within schools, where a small number of teachers and pupils could get to know one another well and work out a way of living that makes sense to them.

I would especially like to see us make available a whole range of alternative programs representing a diversity of educational styles, so that a student and his parents could choose that which best fit his value system — a kind of voucher plan for the selection of alternatives, all under the public umbrella.[9]

Some alternative schools operate as voluntary racial integration models within their communities. In Louisville, Philadelphia, and St. Paul, alternative-school students are admitted in proportion to the racial makeup of the total communities. Forced bussing may become unnecessary in some communities as more families are able to choose from among integrated alternatives.

James S. Coleman has stated:

What I think is needed in the long run is a new and totally different solution to what comprises a school. I would characterize this approach as a breaking apart of the school — where some of the child's activities are carried out in one setting, others in another setting. Some of these activities would be class-integrated, but not all need be. When a child has a diverse array of educational settings, then it's not necessary for every one of those settings to be class-integrated.[10]

Coleman could very well have been describing the St. Paul Learning Centers Program, in which students spend one-half of the day in their neighborhood school and one-half in a racially integrated learning center. To date, over 90 percent of the families who were offered this voluntary program have chosen to have their children participate.[11]

Undoubtedly some will be concerned about the possibility of too much diversity in public education. Certainly we are a long way from this today, but perhaps the words of Bruce Howell, superintendent of the Tulsa Public Schools, will be comforting:

As for me, I see unity through diversity. A diversity in educational design that will permit parents moving from Houston, New York, or Los Angeles to find a curriculum program and an organizational pattern amenable to their thinking. I see absolutely no need for uniformity of organization or standardization of design. There is room in this sprawling system for alternatives and there is a place for the varied educational philosophies of both educator and patron.

To pretend that administration or supervision of these alternatives is an easy task is to display managerial ignorance. Flexibility and diversity are difficult to manage but, to me, the alternative to diversity is educationally untenable. The alternative is standardization and conformity. It is untenable because now we speak of uniqueness and individuality. This mandates alternatives.[12]

THE ECONOMIC POTENTIAL

. . . the link between innovation and survival is vital, now more than ever. The major function of the United States in the last half of this century is to serve as an arsenal of experimentation on every front—artistic, scientific, social, and technological.[13]

Beyond the problems of literacy, poverty, delinquency, and dropouts, there has been little concern with the relationship between public education and the national economy. (Some readers will remember that there was great concern in 1957-58 over the role of education in the national defense.) This lack of concern may have been because during the first half of this century the schools managed to keep pace with the needs of our rapidly developing industrial society.

At the beginning of the century, the country was still predominantly agricultural, and only about 6 percent of our youth finished high school. By the end of World War II the economy was predominantly industrial; we were the world's leading nation in industrial production; and over half of our youth finished high school.

Some of the economic realities of today's world—worldwide inflation, the change in the value of the dollar, and our balance of trade with other nations—are the result of a sudden and at least partially unexpected change in our economy: in less than twenty years our postwar industrial superiority began to decline. We can no longer compete with other advanced industrial nations in the manufacture of goods.

The national economy is moving from industrial production to what Peter Drucker has called "the knowledge sector"[14]—from an industrial society to a society whose basic skill is the development and dissemination of ideas, not products, "a professional, managerial, and technical society" that "will more and more export programmers, consultants, technicians, theses, reports, teachers, lecturers, and art, broadly defined."[15]

Today this "knowledge sector" accounts for one-third of our gross national product; by 1980 it will produce one-half of the gross national product.[16] Economically, we can no longer afford a monolithic system of public education that originated in an agrarian society and developed its present character in an industrial society. The link between educational diversity and an economy based on innovation is obvious. We need alternatives that are responsive to the needs of our "creative minority."[17] If the schools do not nurture and develop creativity and innovation for the future, our country will not be able to compete in the world market of the future.

THE EDUCATIONAL POTENTIAL

Throughout this book we have emphasized that the optional alternative public schools would not replace, but would be complementary to, the conventional schools. Here we will review the ways in which these options will complement the standard educational program within any community.

The first and most obvious way is that alternative schools will be responsive to the needs of some students whose needs are not being met by the existing program. Some children and youth need schools that provide for different styles of learning. Some need smaller schools with more opportunities for decision-making and self-determinism. Some would benefit from more learning experiences out in the community, including work experiences. Some children learn better in open, informal, noncompetitive, or non-print-centered environments. Some will benefit from schools without grade-levels;

others from schools without traditional subjects. Some need more opportunities to develop social skills and social responsibility.

On the opening page of this book, we stated that different people learn in different ways. We don't yet know enough about learning to respond to the learning needs of every child, but we can make a broader range of options available to every child. Recently there has been much interest on the part of educators in this country in the work of Jean Piaget, a Swiss psychologist, investigating the cognitive development of children. Based on his work with Piaget, Furth has suggested that we need schools that develop the thinking (cognitive) skills rather than the reading skills in the early years.[18] Beecher Harris has suggested the need for a school without traditional subjects.[19] The second way the alternatives will complement the system is in providing a structure for learning more about which schools meet the needs of students with different learning styles.

Some research is already underway in this area. Hunt has developed and tried a model for matching the conceptual levels of students with two different learning models (environments).[20] The voluntary nature of the alternative schools overcomes many of the problems related to research with human subjects. Innovations can be explored and pioneered in the smaller alternative schools that might be resisted in the larger conventional school, particularly if all students and teachers were compelled to participate.

Third, the alternative schools will encourage the conventional schools to look at themselves more carefully and more critically. In many communities, there are long waiting lists for admission to the alternative schools. This frequently creates a healthy self-examination on the part of the faculties in the conventional schools.

Fourth, the alternative schools provide for more community involvement in the educational process: through initial dialogue within the community on the need for optional alternatives, through those families who must choose among the optional alternative schools, and through the involvement of community members in the normal routine of the alternative school. The development of optional schools creates a forum for the discussion and analysis of schools and their role in a postindustrial society. In some communities, this forum will lead to cooperative reform efforts.

Every community should consider the need for alternative public schools. Many communities will find the alternatives are needed immediately; many will not. In some communities school administrators will perceive the need for alternatives, but teachers and parents will not. In some communities parents will be the first to perceive the need. And in other communities teachers and students may be first. This dialogue within the community is critical so that parents, teachers, and students will understand, and have a voice in determining, the availability of options. After such a dialogue, a decision that the community has no need for alternative schools at this time is just as healthy and worthwhile as a decision that alternatives are needed.

Fifth, the alternative structure provides a simple mechanism for continuous change and improvement. Already, in some communities, alternatives to the alternatives are being developed and tried. Creating a plurality of parallel structures (alternative schools) within the system provides a structure which is more responsive to learning needs without additional bureaucratic mechanisms.

Red tape, administrative machinery, and all that goes by the name of bureaucracy are the inevitable accompaniments of large-scale organization. They tend to assume such importance as to give the impression that the organization exists for their sake, rather than the other way around. The tendency is toward dehumanization.[21]

Because the alternative schools tend to be smaller than the conventional schools, they represent a return to simpler organizational structures rather than a continued expansion of an already too complex bureaucracy. This simpler structure will make it possible for the alternative school to act as a short-range planning and exploring unit within the system to speed the rate of future educational change. The alternatives can be viewed as an organizational-development strategy to encourage innovation within the system for they will attract those who wish to innovate, whether they be administrators, researchers, teachers, parents, students, or other community members.

Already some alternative schools are developing significantly different curricula. Experts have always recommended that a school's curriculum should be designed to meet local needs. But the trend in the sixties was toward national curricular development. Now some alternatives are bringing the community back into the curriculum. Schools-without-walls, learning centers, and multicultural schools are building closer community-school ties. Students spend more time studying their own community and its problems, and community members spend more time in the school. Students are discovering the relationship between the school's curriculum and the reality of daily life in the community.

Chapter 4 considered the need for curricular reform. The alternative schools are one avenue to a more realistic and effective curriculum for the future. Some alternative schools are developing curricula on environmental education, consumer education, career education, global education, sex education, futures education, parent-family education, citizen-voter education, multicultural education, all of which cut across the boundary lines of traditional subject matter.

Sixth, the alternative schools provide opportunities for exploring, designing, and developing a much broader array of learning facilities. The basic classroom structure of the typical conventional school has changed little over the centuries. Already alternative schools are using a variety of nonconventional facilities available within their communities. The smaller, more flexible school could become a proving ground for new concepts in school design, new combinations of hard and soft space, and totally new approaches to the development of learning environments. Already research is underway attempting to match the learning styles of students with different learning environments.[22]

Seventh, conventional education rewards and allows a limited range of teaching styles. Not all teachers are comfortable within this range. Many of us remember brilliant and gifted teachers who refused to conform and were lost to the profession. Open informal education, currently popular in England and becoming more so here, requires a significantly different teaching style. Some teachers move easily into the open schools; some do not. A plurality of modes of education will provide opportunities for wider variations in teaching styles and for more diversity among teachers and administrators.

The alternatives provide new opportunities for the cooperative development of better teacher-education programs. Has anyone in education ever been satisfied with the education of teachers? The smaller optional school provides a field base for cooperative ventures between the public schools and the teacher-education institutions. Already several universities are working out cooperative programs with alternative schools.

At Indiana University we used to have one monolithic program for the education of elementary and secondary teachers. Today our students may choose from among over twenty alternative programs. One of these programs is a fifth-year internship or residency in alternative public schools. The students spend two summers at I.U. and work as interns or teachers in an alternative public school during the academic year in between. These students are all certificated secondary teachers who are interested in teaching careers in alternative schools. The school district assumes major responsibility for their field training. A public school person, either teacher or administrator, serves as an adjunct professor in charge of the field experiences of the students at each site. This year's field sites included Louisville, Kentucky; Grand Rapids, Michigan; Oak Ridge, Tennessee; Racine, Wisconsin; and Seattle, Washington.

Eighth, and most important of all, is simply the benefits that accrue from providing educational choice within the community. In addition to being more democratic, options also have a psychological advantage over compulsion. There is a natural loyalty and affiliation for that which is chosen over that which is mandated. Choosing involves people. They have to think about the options. The attitudes of the community toward the schools will become more positive as parents see real options available. Teachers and administrators will benefit from a clientele which comes by choice rather than compulsion.

AN IDEA WHOSE TIME HAS COME?

There was a time, not too many years ago, when public opinion changed rather slowly. An idea propounded by an individual or a group and accepted in one part of the community could develop slowly until, perhaps decades later, it received general support. But today, with almost instantaneous communication, the time lag between the first expression of a concept and a national discussion of it is extremely short. If an idea catches on, if it seems desirable to many articulate people, it is but a short step to demands for its instant implementation. Too often, little heed is given to the fact that basic changes cannot be easily made in a highly complex society.[23]

In this book we have tried to present a brief picture of the development of optional alternative public schools, their status today, and their potential for tomorrow. For those who wish a more comprehensive and detailed exploration of the alternative schools movement, a bibliography of recommended readings follows. Only five years ago, I doubt whether we could have found a single reference on the optional alternative public school. Today, we can find hundreds, if not thousands. No one was really pushing them, but here they are. The most powerful and impressive aspect of the alternative public schools is the unbelievably widespread support they have gained in such a short time (as educational changes go). I am forced to conclude that the optional alternative public school is "an idea whose time has come."

AFTERWORD

I can't resist closing with this bizarre report from one of our students, a resident teacher in the Alternative Schools Teacher Education Program, describing a student in a school-within-a-school program.

One student, a girl, had been overweight, unattractive, and apathetic to the extent that she would not even visit with relatives. Within a few months after coming to Blank High School, and her parents say as a direct result of this program, she lost 20 pounds, she began to take an interest in her appearance, she went out and got herself a job babysitting, and she made the honor roll; and her father told us that he had a new problem since boys were beginning to call for the first time.

Notes

CHAPTER 1

1. Charles E. Silberman, *Crisis in the Classroom* (New York: Random House, 1970), p. 332.

2. James Cass, "Where Are We Today?" *Saturday Review/World*, October 9, 1973, p. 43.

3. Shelley Umans, *How to Cut the Cost of Education* (New York: McGraw-Hill, 1973), p. xi.

4. Grace Hechinger, "U.S. Schools Are Number One," *NEA Reporter*, 12:5 (October, 1973), p. 2. Reprinted from the *Wall Street Journal*.

5. Ruth Weinstock, *The Greening of the High School* (New York: Educational Facilities Laboratories, 1973), p. 17.

6. Seymour B. Sarason, *The Culture of the School and the Problem of Change* (Boston: Allyn & Bacon, 1971), p. 29.

7. Russell Kirk, "Need to Educate Gifted," *Bloomington* (Ind.) *Courier-Tribune*, January 6, 1972, p. 10.

8. Quoted in Weinstock, *Greening of the High School*, p. 11.

9. Paul Nachtigal, "Attempts to Change Education in the Sixties," *Changing Schools*, 1:2, p. 8.

10. Dwight Allen, "Alternative Public Schools for the Future," in *Individualized Education* (Minneapolis: Minnesota School Facilities Council, 1971), p. 27.

11. Ivan Illich, *Deschooling Society* (New York: Harper & Row, 1970).

CHAPTER 2

1. Mario D. Fantini in a speech at Vancouver, B.C., August 21, 1973.

2. "Alternative Schools Seek Broader Acceptance," *Education U.S.A.*, October 15, 1973, p. 39.

3. White House Conference on Children, *Report to the President* (Washington: U.S. Government Printing Office, 1970), p. 423.

4. President's Commission on School Finance, *Final Report* (Washington: U.S. Government Printing Office, 1972), p. 76.

5. Ruth Weinstock, *The Greening of the High School* (New York: Educational Facilities Laboratories, 1973).

6. Institute for Educational Development, "Transformation and Substitution: Profound Changes in Educational Institutions and Processes" (New York: Institute for Educational Development, 1972).

7. Greg Pinney, "Board Approves Alternative Schools," *Minneapolis Tribune*, March 14, 1973.

8. John Bremer and Michael von Moschzisker, *The School without Walls* (New York: Holt, Rinehart & Winston, 1971), p. 178.

CHAPTER 4

1. Vincent Pinto, "Mother Jones and Her Children's Crusade," *Today/ The Philadelphia Inquirer*, November 18, 1972, p. 17.

2. Glenys G. Unruh, "Beyond Sputnik," *Educational Leadership*, 30:7 (April, 1973), p. 587.

3. Ruth Weinstock, *The Greening of the High School* (New York: Educational Facilities Laboratories, 1973), p. 17.

4. James Agee and Walker Evans, *Let Us Now Praise Famous Men* (New York: Ballantine Books, 1966), pp. 265-66.

5. "Sex on the Airways: Congress Is Aroused," *Saturday Review of the Arts* 1:4 (April 7, 1973), p. 70.

6. Ibid.

7. June Brody, *New York Times*, March 1, 1973. Quoted in *Councilgrams* 34:3 (May, 1973), p. 37.

8. Weinstock, *Greening of the High School*, p. 19.

9. Gillian Tindall, "Death as a Taboo Subject," *Manchester Guardian*. Reprinted in the *Bloomington* (Ind.) *Courier-Tribune*, June 21, 1972, p. 10.

10. David Burmester, "The Language of Deceit," *Media and Methods*, May, 1973, p. 22.

11. "Child-Beating Worse than Watergate," *Bloomington* (Ind.) *Herald-Telephone*, June 26, 1973, p. 10.

12. B. Frank Brown, "Rationale for Change," Keynote Speech, Annual Summer Conference for Indiana Junior and Senior High Principals, Indiana University, July 25, 1973.

13. National Commission on the Reform of Secondary Education, *The Reform of Secondary Education* (New York: McGraw-Hill, 1973), p. 120.

14. Ibid., p. 117.

15. Jeb Magruder, from his testimony before the Ervin Committee, *Bloomington* (Ind.) *Herald-Telephone*, p. 10.

16. Quoted in *Bloomington* (Ind.) *Courier-Tribune* June 14, 1973, p. 8.

17. "Everybody's Doing It," Editorial, *Bloomington* (Ind.) *Herald-Telephone*, September 4, 1973, p. 8.

18. "'Shots' Turn into Nightmare for Kids," *Bloomington* (Ind.) *Courier-Tribune*, June 27, 1973, p. 8.

19. Burmester, "Language of Deceit," p. 22.

20. Jerome Agel, "Monologue with Future Shock," *The Last Supplement to the Whole Earth Catalog*, March, 1971, p. 89.

21. Harold Benjamin, *The Saber-Tooth Curriculum* (New York: McGraw-Hill, 1939), p. 33.

22. Ibid., p. 111.

23. Margaret Mead, "Thinking Ahead," in *Selected Educational Heresies*, ed. W. R. O'Neill (Glenview, Ill.: Scott, Foresman, 1969), p. 362.

24. James S. Coleman, quoted in "PSAC: Last Hurrah from Panel on Youth," by John Walsh, *Science,* October 12, 1973, p. 141.

25. Peter F. Drucker, *The Age of Discontinuity* (New York: Harper & Row, 1968), p. 337.

26. James S. Coleman, "The Children Have Outgrown the Schools," *Psychology Today,* February, 1972, p. 72.

27. James Herndon, *How to Survive in Your Native Land* (New York: Simon & Schuster, 1971), p. 117.

28. Coleman, "The Children Have Outgrown The Schools," pp. 74-75.

29. Weinstock, *Greening of the High School,* p. 31.

CHAPTER 5

1. Mario D. Fantini, "Schools for the Seventies: Institutional Reform," *Today's Education,* April, 1970, p. 43.

2. From a symposium announcement, Research for Better Schools, Inc., Philadelphia, 1973.

3. Mario D. Fantini and Milton A. Young, *Designing Education for Tomorrow's Cities* (New York: Holt, Rinehart & Winston, 1970), p. ix.

4. Jerome S. Bruner, "The Process of Education Revisited," *Phi Delta Kappan,* 53:1 (September, 1971), p. 20.

5. Peter Schrag, "End of the Impossible Dream," *Saturday Review,* September 19, 1970, p. 68.

6. Paul Nachtigal, "Attempts to Change Education in the Sixties," *Changing Schools,* 1:2, p. 8.

7. Paul Nachtigal, *A Foundation Goes to School* (New York: Ford Foundation, 1972), p. 26.

8. Schrag, "End of the Impossible Dream," p. 69.

9. *Education Summary,* February 1, 1974, p. 4.

10. Seymour B. Sarason, *The Culture of the School and the Problem of Change* (Boston: Allyn & Bacon, 1971), p. 212.

11. Harold G. Shane, "A Curriculum Continuum: Possible Trends in the 70's," *Phi Delta Kappan* (March, 1970), p. 389.

12. James Herndon, *How to Survive in Your Native Land* (New York: Simon & Schuster, 1971), pp. 100-101.

13. John I. Goodlad, *The Future of Learning and Teaching* (Washington: National Education Association, 1968), p. 19.

14. John Goodlad and M. Frances Klein, *Behind the Classroom Door* (Belmont, Calif.: Wadsworth, 1970), p. 107.

15. James Guthrie and Paula Skene, "The Escalation of Pedagogical Politics," *Phi Delta Kappan,* 54:6 (February, 1973), p. 387.

16. John I. Goodlad, "Direction and Redirection for Curriculum Change," in *Curriculum Change: Direction and Process* (Washington: Association for Supervision & Curriculum Development, 1966), p. 4.

17. John H. Fischer, "Who Needs Schools?" *Saturday Review*, September 19, 1970, p. 79.

18. Goodlad and Klein, *Behind the Classroom Door*, p. 103.

19. John Goodlad with Renata Von Stoephasius and M. Frances Klein, *The Changing School Curriculum* (New York: Ford Foundation, 1966), p. 11.

20. John I. Goodlad, *The Future of Learning and Teaching* (Washington: National Education Association, 1968), p. 8.

21. Goodlad and Klein, *Behind the Classroom Door*, p. 97.

22. Ibid., p. 99.

23. John I. Goodlad, "The Future of Learning: Into the 21st Century," *AACTE Bulletin*, 24:1 (March, 1971), pp. 4-5. Excerpted from a speech, White House Conference on Children, December, 1970.

24. Benjamin Rossner and Patricia M. Kay, "Will the Promise of C/PBTE Be Fulfilled?" *Phi Delta Kappan*, 55:5 (January, 1974), pp. 291-92.

25. Vincent J. Glennon, "What Happened to the New Math?" *Learning*, October, 1973, p. 66.

CHAPTER 6

1. Neil Postman, "Alternative Education in the Seventies," *The Last Supplement to the Whole Earth Catalog*, March, 1971, p. 41.

2. Charles Silberman, "Charles Silberman on Alternatives to Crisis," *AACTE Bulletin*, 24:1 (March, 1971), p. 8.

3. David L. Clark, "Options—Success or Failure?" *NASSP Bulletin*, 57:374 (September, 1973), pp. 1-2.

4. *The Reform of Secondary Education: A Report of the National Commission on the Reform of Secondary Education* (New York: McGraw-Hill, 1973), p. 109.

5. *Prefaces to Liberty: Selected Writings of John Stuart Mill*, ed. Bernard Wishy (Boston: Beacon Press, 1959), p. 356.

6. Peter Schrag, "End of the Impossible Dream," *Saturday Review*, September 19, 1970, pp. 92-93.

7. Neil Postman and Charles Weingartner, *The Soft Revolution* (New York: Dell, 1971), pp. 12-13.

8. Bruce R. Joyce, "Curriculum and Humanistic Education: 'Monolism' vs. 'Pluralism,'" in *Radical School Reform*, ed. Cornelius J. Troost (Boston: Little, Brown, 1973), p. 250.

9. Thomas Sobol, "The Broader Meaning of Articulation," *Phi Delta Kappan*, 53:1 (September, 1971), p. 29.

10. James S. Coleman, "Class Integration—A Fundamental Break with the Past," *Saturday Review*, May 27, 1972, p. 59.

11. Firmin Alexander, "Integration through Alternatives," *Changing Schools*, 1:3, pp. 2-10.

12. Bruce Howell, *Superintendent's Bulletin*, 44:2 (September 4, 1973), p. 1. (Tulsa Public Schools.)

13. Douglas Davis, "The Soft-Sell," *Newsweek*, July 23, 1973, p. 11.

14. Ibid.

15. Ibid.

16. Ibid.

17. Ibid.

18. Hans Furth, *Piaget for Teachers* (Englewood Cliffs, N.J.: Prentice-Hall, 1970), p. 145.

19. Beecher H. Harris, "Schools without Subjects?" *Educational Leadership*, 29:5 (February, 1972), pp. 420-23.

20. David E. Hunt, *Matching Models in Education* (Toronto: Ontario Institute for Studies in Education, 1971).

21. Robert M. Hutchins, *The Learning Society* (New York: Mentor Books, 1968), pp. 145-46.

22. Hunt, *Matching Models in Education*.

23. L. L. L. Golden, "Public Relations: Alerting Management," *Saturday Review*, September 11, 1971, p. 70.

Bibliography

ON EDUCATIONAL CHANGE

GOODLAD, JOHN I.; KLEIN, M. FRANCES; et al. *Behind the Classroom Door.* Belmont, Calif.: Wadsworth, 1970. This book details a study of classrooms in sixty-seven selected elementary schools after a decade of educational reform. One of the many important conclusions of the study was that the changes believed to be taking place in schools were not getting to the classroom.

KATZ, MICHAEL B. *Class, Bureaucracy, and Schools: The Illusion of Educational Change in America.* New York: Praeger, 1971.

_____ (ed.) *School Reform: Past and Present.* Boston: Little, Brown, 1971. The two books by Katz provide an excellent historical overview of the development of American education and of significant attempts at reform.

NACHTIGAL, PAUL. *A Foundation Goes to School.* New York: Ford Foundation, 1972. This is a report on a field study of twenty-five school projects which the Ford Foundation funded with over $30 million in its Comprehensive School Improvement Program in the sixties. Nachtigal's report and conclusions are generalizable to most of the other reform attempts in that decade and to many in progress today.

National Commission on the Reform of Secondary Education. *The Reform of Secondary Education.* New York: McGraw-Hill, 1973. This report is sure to have an impact on secondary schools in this decade. As one of its many recommendations, it urges the development of alternative public schools in every community.

POSTMAN, NEIL, and WEINGARTNER, CHARLES. *The Soft Revolution.* New York: Dell, 1971. This book, addressed to students, contains many suggestions for improving the schools and making them more humane.

RIST, RAY C. *Restructuring American Education: Innovations and Alternatives.* New Brunswick, N.J.: Transaction Books, 1972. This is a collection of recent essays on innovations within the system and alternatives to the conventional school.

SARASON, SEYMOUR B. *The Culture of the School and the Problem of Change.* Boston: Allyn & Bacon, 1971. This is a thorough analysis of the culture of the conventional school and the problems involved in reform attempts.

WEINSTOCK, RUTH. *The Greening of the High School.* New York: Educational Facilities Laboratories, 1973. This conference report paints a grim picture of the American high school in 1973. All who are concerned about, complacent about, or connected with secondary education should read this.

ON OPTIONAL ALTERNATIVE PUBLIC SCHOOLS

Alternative High Schools: Some Pioneer Programs. Educational Research Service Circular No. 4, 1972. Washington: American Association of School Administrators and National Education Association Research Division.

Alternative Schools: Pioneering Districts Create Options for Students. Education U.S.A. Special Report. Arlington, Va.: National School Public Relations Association, 1972.

More Options: Alternatives to Conventional School. Curriculum Report, 3:2, March, 1973. Washington: National Association of Secondary School Principals.

The three above reports provide background material on, and illustrations of, alternative public schools.

BREMER, JOHN, and VON MOSCHZISKER, MICHAEL. *The School without Walls: Philadelphia's Parkway Program.* New York: Holt, Rinehart & Winston, 1971. Bremer, Parkway's first director, describes the planning and development of Parkway, the prototype of the school-without-walls.

FANTINI, MARIO D. *Public Schools of Choice: A Plan for the Reform of American Education.* New York: Simon & Schuster, 1973. Fantini, long a leader in attempts to improve the schools, presents his comprehensive plan for the development of optional public schools. This book is "must" reading for advocates of alternative public schools and for those who are seeking more information on them.

HERNDON, JAMES. *How to Survive in Your Native Land.* New York: Simon & Schuster, 1971. This is an amusing description of an attempt to create a school-within-a-school, but read it also for its exposure of conventional practices.

NASSP Bulletin: Alternatives in Public Education: Movement or Fad? 57:374, September, 1973.

National Elementary Principal: The Great Alternatives Hassle, 52:6, April, 1973.

Phi Delta Kappan: Alternative Schools, 54:7, March, 1973. These three 1973 journal issues were devoted to the development of alternative public schools. There is a host of articles in each—both pro and con.

RIORDAN, ROBERT. *Alternative Schools in Action.* Bloomington, Ind.: Phi Delta Kappa Educational Foundation, 1972. This brief PDK fastback says a lot about alternative schools and their problems, particularly the Cambridge Pilot School, where the author teaches.

ON OPEN EDUCATION

NYQUIST, EWALD, and HAWES, GENE. *Open Education: A Sourcebook for Parents and Teachers.* New York: Bantam Books, 1972.

PERRONE, VITO. *Open Education: Promise and Problems.* Bloomington, Ind.: Phi Delta Kappa Educational Foundation, 1972.

RATHBONE, CHARLES (ed.). *Open Education: The Informal Classroom.* New York: Citation Press, 1971.

SILBERMAN, CHARLES (ed.). *The Open Classroom Reader.* New York: Vintage Books, 1972. These four books provide excellent introductions to the field of open education.

OTHER

HUNT, DAVID E. *Matching Models in Education: The Coordination of Teaching Methods with Student Characteristics.* Toronto: Ontario Institute for Studies in Education, 1971.

JOYCE, BRUCE, and WEIL, MARCIA. *Models of Teaching.* Englewood Cliffs, N.J.: Prentice-Hall, 1972. These two books are only for those who are relatively sophisticated in educational research. They describe the attempts underway to begin to match teaching and environment to the learning style of the student.